TRUE STORIES OF
THE FIRST
WORLD WAR

First published in 2004 by Usborne Publishing Ltd,
Usborne House, 83-85 Saffron Hill,
London EC1N 8RT, England.
www.usborne.com

A catalogue record for this title is available from the British Library.

ISBN 0 7460 5749 0
American ISBN 07945 07212

Printed in Great Britain

Designed by Sarah Cronin
Illustrated by John Woodcock
Edited by Jane Chisholm and Rosie Dickins
Cover photograph © Hulton Archive/GettyImages
Cover design by Glen Bird

With grateful thanks to Terry Charman, of the Imperial War Museum,
London, for his most helpful comments on the manuscript.

TRUE STORIES OF
THE FIRST
WORLD WAR

PAUL DOWSWELL

CONTENTS

Over by Christmas?

1914

In the first four days of August 1914, the world's most powerful nations declared war on each other. They lined up in two opposing camps. On one side was Germany and Austria-Hungary, who were known as the Central Powers. On the other was Britain and France, together with their empires, and Russia. They were known as the Allies. In the course of the war, other nations would be drawn into the conflict, too. The Ottoman empire and Bulgaria joined the Central Powers. Italy, Romania, Japan and China joined the Allies. So did the United States, despite the initial reluctance of a great many of its people. It was to be the first real world war - in that it involved countries from every inhabited continent - although most of the fighting took place on what became known as the Western and Eastern fronts, on either side of Germany.

As news of the outbreak of war spread, crowds began to gather in the hot summer sunshine, congregating in the great squares and parks of Europe's principal cities. Far from being fearful or anxious, they were elated — like football fans anticipating a closely-fought game. Each side expected a war of great marches and heroic battles, quickly decided. The German emperor, the kaiser, told his troops they would be home before the leaves fell from the trees. The British were not so optimistic, although it was frequently claimed that the war would be over by Christmas. Only a few far-sighted politicians realized what was coming, including the British foreign secretary, Sir Edward Grey.

Watching the dusk from his window on August 4, the day Britain declared war on Germany, Sir Edward sighed: "The lamps are going out all over Europe; we shall not see them lit again in our lifetime." His melancholy remark had a deep resonance, for the world would never be the same. Grey and his fellow citizens were living in a strong and prosperous country, with a vast empire. The war would provide a rude awakening to the grimier reality of the 20th century, completely undermining Britain's position as the world's most powerful nation.

Almost all the other participants in the war suffered a similar reversal of fortune, or worse. In France, half of all men aged between 20 and 35 were killed or badly wounded; its eminent position in the world would never recover. The Austro-Hungarian empire collapsed, with repercussions that can still be seen in the squabbling Balkan nations of today. The Germans ended the war on the brink of a communist revolution, and lost their own monarchy. The war swept away the Russian monarchy too, then brought

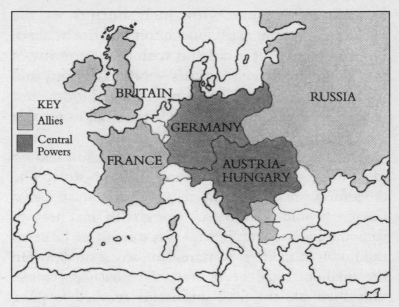

The Allies and Central Powers at the start of the war

the communist Bolsheviks to power. With them came 70 years of brutal, totalitarian oppression. Like many countries in Eastern Europe, the Russians have never really recovered from the First World War, and its awful consequences. Only the United States did well out of it. By 1919, it had become the richest, most powerful nation on Earth, and was set to dominate the 20th century.

Quite apart from its consequences, there is something uniquely haunting about the First World War. The Second World War was far worse in terms of its cost in human life: it claimed over four times as many victims. It was also fought with much greater brutality, and came with such horrors as the Holocaust and the mass destruction of cities by aerial bombardment. But it did end with the overthrow of two undoubtedly evil regimes – Nazi Germany and Imperial Japan – and a peace which lasted for the rest of the century. The First World War, for all its terrible cost, produced no positive results at all.

The city crowds that gathered that August had no idea what the next four years had in store. The dreadful waste of life – what British statesman Lloyd George would describe as "the ghastly butchery of vain and insane offensives" – was something hitherto unknown in modern warfare. But, worst of all, when the final shell had been fired, the final gas canister unleashed and the final submarine recalled to port, there was nothing to show for it except an awful air of unfinished business and a tally of 21 million dead. Novelist H.G. Wells called it "the war that will end war", and the phrase had caught on. It was such a gut-wrenchingly horrible conflict, everyone hoped humanity would not be foolish enough to do it again. The Versailles peace treaty officially ended the war in 1919. One of the leading participants, French commander Marshal Foch, dismissed the proceedings as "a 20-year cease-fire". He was exactly right. By the early 1920s, people had already begun to refer to "the war that will end war" as the *First* World War.

The causes of the war were many. A system of rival alliances between the different European powers had built up in the previous decades, as individual countries tried to bolster their security and ambitions with powerful allies. But, although alliances provided some security, they also came with obligations. The events that led to war were set in motion in June 1914, when a Serbian student named Gavrilo Princip assassinated the heir to the Austro-Hungarian throne, Archduke Franz Ferdinand. In retaliation, Austria-Hungary swiftly declared war on Serbia. But Serbia was an ally of Russia's. So Russia joined the war against Austria-Hungary, and all the other rival nations, tied to their respective alliances, were dragged into the conflict – whether they wanted to be or not.

But why should a quarrel between Russia and Austria-Hungary over a little-known country in Eastern Europe automatically involve France, Germany and Britain? It was because each was obliged to support the other in the event of war. And there were other long-standing resentments, too. Britain, then the world's greatest empire, maintained her power by means of the world's greatest fleet. So when Germany began to build a fleet to rival the Royal Navy, relations between the two countries deteriorated sharply. The British and French both had vast colonial empires. Germany, similarly prosperous and powerful, had very few colonies and wanted more. They all joined in the fighting to maintain or improve their position in the world.

The reason the conflict was so horrific is easier to

explain. The war occurred at a moment in the evolution of military technology when weapons to defend a position were much more effective than the weapons available to attack it. The previous 50 years had seen the development of trench fortifications, barbed wire, machine guns, and rapid-fire rifles. All of this made it simple and straightforward for an army defending its territory. But an army attacking well-defended territory had to rely on its infantrymen, armed with only rifles and bayonets – and they were to be slaughtered in their millions.

Yet all the generals involved in the war had been trained to fight by attacking, so that is what they did. They had also been trained to think of cavalry as one of their greatest offensive weapons. The cavalry – still armed with lances, as they had been for the previous 2,000 years – took part in a few battles, particularly at the start of the war. But these elite troops were quickly massacred. The tactics of Alexander the Great, Ghengiz Khan and Napoleon, all of whom had used cavalry to great effect, were no match for the industrial-scale killing power of the 20th-century machine gun.

There were other ugly additions to the new technology of warfare: poisonous gas, fighter and bomber aircraft, zeppelins, tanks, submarines and, especially, artillery (field guns, howitzers etc.). Armies had long used cannons but, by the time of the First World War, these weapons had reached a new pinnacle of sophistication. They were much more accurate and fired more rapidly than they had done. The shells they fired contained high explosives, shrapnel (metal balls) or gas. Over 70% of all casualties in the First World War were caused by artillery. As artillery could be used both to attack and defend, it gave neither side an advantage. It simply gouged up the battlefield landscape, making fighting even more difficult and dangerous for the hapless participants.

The war began with a massive German attack on France, known as the Schlieffen Plan after its originator, General Alfred Graf von Schlieffen. The plan called for the German army to wheel through neutral Belgium and seize Paris. The idea was to knock France out of the war as soon as possible. Apart from neutralizing one of Germany's most powerful rivals, this would have two other advantages. First, it would deprive Britain of a base on the continent from which to attack Germany. Second, with their enemies to the west conquered or severely disadvantaged, Germany could then concentrate on defeating the much larger Russian army to the east.

The fighting in late summer and early autumn of 1914 was among the fiercest of the war. Both sides suffered huge losses. At the Battle of the Marne, the German advance was halted less than 24km (15 miles) from Paris. By November, the armies had become bogged down in opposing rows of trenches,

Map of Europe showing the main fronts in 1914

which stretched from the English Channel down to the Swiss border. Give or take the odd few miles here and there, the front line would remain much the same for the next four years.

On Germany's eastern border, its armies won crushing victories against vast hordes of invading Russian troops, at Tannenberg in late August, and the Masurian lakes in early September. They had prevented the "Russian steamroller" from overrunning their country. From here on, the German army would gradually advance eastwards.

In 1915, there was an attempt by British and ANZAC (Australian and New Zealand Army Corps) troops to attack the Central Powers from the south, via Gallipoli in Turkey. The strategy was a disaster. Between April and December 1915, around 200,000 men were killed trying to gain a foothold in this narrow, hilly peninsular.

By 1916, the war that was supposed to have ended by Christmas 1914 looked as if it would last forever. Determined, in his own words, "to bleed the French army white", the German chief-of-staff, General Erich von Falkenhayn, launched an attack on the fortresses of Verdun in February. His strategy was a success in some ways. The French army lost 350,000 men, and never really recovered. But Falkenhayn's own troops suffered 330,000 casualties too, and the French held on to their fortresses. Von Falkenhayn was relieved of his command.

Meanwhile, on May 31, 1916, the German High Seas Fleet challenged the British Royal Navy in the North Sea, at the Battle of Jutland. In an all-out confrontation, 14 British ships, and 11 German ships were lost. If the British navy had been destroyed, then Germany would undoubtedly have won the war. Island Britain would have been starved into submission, as cargo ships would have been unable to sail into British waters without being sunk. The British may have lost more ships at Jutland, but the German navy never ventured out to sea again, and the British naval blockade of Germany remained intact. A pattern was emerging, of titanic struggles, vast casualties, and almost indifferent results. Worse was to come.

On July 1, 1916, another great battle began. The British launched an all-out attack on the Somme, in northern France. The British commander-in-chief, Field Marshal Haig, was convinced that a massive assault would break the German front line. This would enable him to send in his cavalry, and allow his troops to make a considerable advance into enemy territory. The attack, known as "the Big Push", failed in the first few minutes and 20,000 men were slaughtered in a single morning. Yet the Battle of the Somme dragged on for a further five miserable months.

By 1917, a numb despair had settled on the fighting nations. With appalling stubbornness, Field Marshal Haig launched another attack on the German lines – this time at Passchendaele, in Belgium. Bad weather turned the battlefield into an impenetrable mudbath. Between July 31 and November 10, when the assault was finally called off, both sides had lost a quarter of a million men.

Two other events in 1917 had massive consequences for the outcome of the war. The Russian people had suffered terribly and, in March, a revolution forced Tsar Nicholas II to abdicate. In November, the radical Bolsheviks seized power and imposed a communist dictatorship on their country.

One of the first things they did was to make peace with Germany. The Bolsheviks assumed, incorrectly, that similar revolutions would soon sweep through Europe, especially Germany. So, believing that Germany would soon be a fellow communist regime who would treat Russia more fairly, they agreed to a very disadvantageous peace treaty at Brest-Litovsk in March 1918. Germany took vast tracts of land from the Russian empire – including Poland, the Ukraine, the Baltic states and Finland. For Germany, this was a great victory. Not only had they added a vast chunk of territory to their eastern border, they could now concentrate all their forces on defeating the British and French.

But, despite their successes, events were conspiring against Germany. After the Battle of Jutland had failed to win them dominance of the seas, Germany had drifted into a policy of "unrestricted" submarine warfare. This meant that German U-boats would attack any ship heading for Britain – even those belonging to neutral nations. It was a tremendously effective strategy, but it backfired disastrously. The submarine attacks caused outrage overseas, especially in the USA, and became one of the main reasons America turned against Germany. President Woodrow Wilson brought his country in on the side of the Allies on April 6, 1917, but it wasn't until the summer of 1918 that American troops began to arrive on the Western Front in great numbers.

The timing could not have been worse for the German army. The Ludendorff Offensive, named after German commander Erich Ludendorff, began on March 21, 1918. Forty-six divisions broke through weary British and French troops on the Somme, and swept on to Paris. For a while, it looked as if Germany would win the war on the Western Front as well as the Eastern Front. So alarmed were the British that Field Marshal Haig issued an order to his troops on April 12, commanding them to stand and fight until they were killed: "With our backs to the wall and believing in the justice of our cause each one of us must fight to the end," it said.

But the Ludendorff Offensive turned out to be the last desperate fling of a dying army. Faced with stubborn British resistance, and fresh and eager American troops, the German advance ground to a halt. The German army had no more to give. At home, the German population, starved after four years of blockade by the Royal Navy, was on the verge of a revolution. In August 1918, the Allies made a massive breakthrough against the German front lines in northern France, and began an inexorable push towards the German border. Facing mutiny among his armed forces, revolution at home, and an inevitable invasion of home territory, the kaiser abdicated and the German government called for an armistice – a cease-fire. The time was set to be 11:00am on November 11, 1918. Fighting continued right up to the final seconds.

In his memoirs, General Ludendorff recalled the situation with anguish: "[By] 9 November, Germany, lacking any firm guidance, bereft of all will, robbed of her princes, collapsed like a pack of cards. All that we had lived for, all that we had bled four long years to maintain, was gone."

Although there were wild celebrations in Allied cities, many of the soldiers on the Western Front took the news with a weary shrug. "We read in the papers of the tremendous celebrations in London and Paris, but could not bring ourselves to raise even a cheer," wrote one New Zealand artillery man. "The only feeling we had was one of great relief."

The guns fell silent. Grasses, weeds and vines gradually crept over the desolate battlefields, covering the withered trees and ravaged fields, and turning the blackened earth to a pleasanter green. Crude, makeshift burial grounds were replaced by towering monuments and magnificent cemeteries. Many of those killed found a final resting place among long rows of marble crosses, each with a name, rank and date of death engraved upon it. Others, whose torn remains were incomplete and unrecognizable, were buried under crosses marked "known unto God".

It would be another 10 or 15 years before the charred trucks, shell carriages and tanks were taken away for scrap, and the shell holes filled in. By the time war broke out again in 1939, much of the land was being farmed again; but the faint smell of gas still lingered in corners and copses, rusting rifles and helmets still littered the scarred ground, and shell cases, shrapnel fragments and bones could still be tilled from the battlefields of northern France and Belgium – as they can to this day.

The Angels of Mons

September 1914

It was early afternoon on August 24, 1914. Captain Arthur Osborn of the 4th Dragoon Guards had had a nightmare couple of weeks. Now, waiting to intercept units of German cavalry, he looked at the thundery sky and was reminded of a verse from Revelation 12 in the Bible: "And the great dragon was cast out… and his angels were cast out with him." His present surroundings added nothing to his mood. He was in the Belgian mining town of Mons, a marshy area intersected with canals, and littered with towering slag heaps. He and his companions in the British Expeditionary Force (BEF) had been sent to France at the outbreak of war. Facing him, and the other British, French and Belgian troops, were one and a half million German soldiers, hellbent on reaching Paris as part of General Schlieffen's strategy to win a quick victory.

In between marching for days on end, Osborn and his men faced moments of terror when they were caught by advance German units or artillery fire. When their generals commanded them to stand and fight, they confronted hordes of enemy soldiers, advancing in ranks so thick, they seemed to resemble dark clouds sweeping though the green fields towards them. A soldier fighting in such conditions reaches a condition of exhaustion unimaginable to most people. In such a state, men reported seeing imaginary castles on the horizon, towering giants or squadrons of charging cavalry in the far distance – all, of course, hallucinations.

The losses the British troops were taking were disastrous – an average BEF infantry battalion of 850 men would be left with barely 30 by the time the German advance had been halted and the trenches set up. Osborn, and many others like him, could not help but feel they were living in apocalyptic times. It was during their desperate retreat that one of the strangest stories of the war arose: it was whispered that a host of angels had come to the aid of British troops at Mons. Not only had the angels saved the soldiers from certain death, but they had also struck down the attacking Germans. Extraordinary though the story was, it was widely believed for decades after the war ended.

During the early stages of the fighting, the army authorities allowed no real news out from the battlefield and, in consequence, wild and fanciful stories began to circulate. War correspondent Philip Gibbs wrote that the press and public were so desperate to know what was happening that "any scrap of description, any glimmer of truth, and wild statement, rumour, fairy tale or deliberate lie, which reached them from France or Belgium" was readily accepted. "The liars had a great time," he reflected.

In this feverish atmosphere, the story of the Angels of Mons began to circulate among the British public. Like all urban legends, it was always told second-hand – a friend of a friend had learned... a friend had heard of a letter from the front which mentioned... an anonymous officer had reported... The legend blossomed. Sometimes a mysterious, glowing cloud featured in the story, sometimes it was a band of ghostly horsemen or archers, or even Joan of Arc. But most of the time it was a host of angels, that had come to rescue the beleaguered British troops.

Many wild stories from this time were the result of government propaganda, but the origin of this one was more innocent. It was a newspaper article in the September 29 edition of the *London Evening News*, written by freelance journalist Arthur Machen. A fanciful and rather opaque piece of fiction, it tells of a group of British soldiers at Mons, under attack by a vast phalanx of German troops. As the Germans advance towards them, and death seems moments away, one of the soldiers mutters the motto *Adsit Anglis Sanctus Georgius* – May St. George be present help to the English. Just then, according to the story:

"the roar of battle died down in his ears to a gentle murmur... [then] he heard, or seemed to hear thousands shouting 'St. George! St. George!' And as the soldier heard these voices he saw before him, beyond the trench, a long line of shapes, with a shining about them. They were like men who drew the bow, and with another shout, their cloud of arrows flew singing and tingling through the air towards the German host [a large group of soldiers]."

The story had a potent mixture: England's patron saint and ghostly bowmen, the spirits of those archers, perhaps, who had won a famous English victory against the French at Agincourt in 1415. Perhaps the fiction was believed to be true because it appeared in the news section of the paper – probably due to problems fitting it elsewhere, or a simple misunderstanding by a designer on the paper, rather than any deliberate attempt by the *Evening News* to mislead its readers. The original tale was preposterous enough but, in the weeks and months after it was printed, the retellings became even more fanciful. British newspapers stoked the strange hysteria by reproducing illustrations showing pious British troops praying in their trench, as ranks of ghostly bowmen pour down deadly, glowing arrows on the approaching Germans. As it swept through the country, the tale evolved, with the bowmen becoming angel archers instead.

Machen never claimed his story had a grain of

truth to it. "The tale is mere and sheer invention," he freely admitted. "I made it all up out of my own head." He was extremely embarrassed at the effect it had on the British public. But the authenticity of the story was still being debated decades after the war ended. In the late 1920s, one American paper carried a report quoting a German officer who declared the angels were actually motion picture images projected onto the clouds by aircraft. The idea, said the officer, had been to spread terror among the British soldiers, but the plan had backfired badly when the British assumed the ghostly figures were on their side. Curiously, this report took it for granted that the angels had appeared; it was merely offering a logical, if extremely implausible, explanation for why they were seen. And even in the 1970s and 80s, Britain's Imperial War Museum was still being asked about the authenticity of the story.

Nowadays, it is easy to scoff at the naiveté of those who believed such stories. But the fact that the tale was so widely believed tells us much about the society that fought the war. Captain Osborn, who appears at the start of this chapter, was lucky enough to survive, but thousands of other men had been killed in the opening months of the conflict. For those who had lost husbands or sons, there was a great need for consolation. Stories like the Angels of Mons brought reassurance to grieving relatives. For them, it was especially pleasing to note that God was so obviously on the side of the British, rather than the Germans.

Other unlikely stories continued to circulate throughout the war. Some were based on the usual far-fetched tales told by troops on leave from the trenches. It was widely believed, for example, that a renegade, international band of deserters ran loose in No Man's Land, the territory that lay between the opposing trenches. Other stories were deliberately fabricated by a British government propaganda unit, to bolster morale at home and also to lure America into the war on the side of the Allies.

In fact, for most of the time, German military forces behaved no better or worse than any other army. But, during the desperate early stage of the war, the German army had dealt brutally with any resistance from Belgian civilians to the invasion of their country – hostages were shot and villages massacred in reprisals. From the bones of such stories, British propaganda built a picture of the entire German people as a nation of godless barbarians. "Huns" was the term most often used, after the 4th-century soldiers of Attila, who had laid waste Rome and much of Italy.

Sometimes, this propaganda was almost ridiculous in its grotesque imagery. German soldiers, it was reported, had replaced the bells in Belgian church steeples with hanging nuns. Later in the war, stories were planted in the British press saying that the Germans had their own corpse factory, and that

German soldiers killed in the fighting were sent there, so their bodies could be made into explosives, candles, industrial lubricants and boot polish.

The reaction such stories produced in Britain was sometimes equally bizarre. German dachshund dogs were stoned in the street. Shops with German immigrant owners were attacked and looted. The British royal family changed their German name of Saxe-Coburg-Gotha to Windsor. But mainly the stories created an atmosphere of intense fear and hatred of the enemy – as they were intended to do. Many of those who rushed to join the army in the opening months of the war were convinced they were fighting for civilization against a barbaric foe who would rape and mutilate their wives and children, should they ever cross the channel and invade Britain.

After the war, people realized that much of the news concerning the war, and their German enemy, had been outright lies. Newspapers would never be so openly trusted again. This attitude still persisted during the Second World War. This meant that in the early stages of that war, when stories of German death camps first broke, they were widely disbelieved. It was too much of an echo of the corpse factory story from 20 years before.

Strange meetings

December 1914

For most people, Christmas is a time of celebration – presents to be opened with family and friends, heaps of rich food and drink, and optimism for the New Year. So imagine the feelings of men exhausted from four months of heavy fighting: homesick, missing their wives and children, and spending Christmas Eve shivering in muddy, waterlogged trenches. Their lives seemed to be lived out in a dark looking-glass world of cold, hunger and hatred. But Christmas sometimes works a strange magic, even in conditions like these, as it did in the December of 1914.

On Christmas Eve, the German guns on the Western Front fell silent soon after dark. No shells, no murderous chatter of machine gun fire, not even the occasional whine of a sniper's bullet. The British soldiers followed their example. It was a cold, clear night, and stars burned brightly in the sky. The utter silence that fell over the trenches created an eerie atmosphere. Then, along some sections of the trenches, lookouts on the British side saw strange lights flickering and swinging along the German front line. Some shots were fired. But, when officers peered through their trench periscopes or binoculars, they were amazed to see that these lights were illuminated Christmas decorations. There were even some small Christmas trees hung with candles. At first, many soldiers remained suspicious. After all, the British commander-in-chief, Field Marshal French, had issued a stern order to all units warning of a German attack over Christmas or New Year. "Special vigilance will be maintained during these periods," they had been told.

Then the German soldiers started singing carols. Some were unfamiliar to the British soldiers, but others, such as *"Stille Nacht"* (Silent Night), were very well known to them. Then the British soldiers began to sing carols too, the two sides serenading each other with shared Christmas memories. Perhaps it was hearing these familiar songs that led to the amazing events of the following day.

Dawn on Christmas morning brought a thick mist over some sections of the Front but, when it cleared, the most extraordinary scene revealed itself. All along No Man's Land, in some places almost as far as the eye could see, soldiers had ventured out to meet their enemies. They huddled around in small groups, usually based around one man who could speak the other side's language. Sometimes, French was the common language between them. Sometimes, men spoke no language at all, communicating with smiles and gestures. Soldiers swapped cigarettes, chocolate and beer or whiskey. Others, more daringly, exchanged items of equipment – belt buckles, regimental badges, even helmets. Before the war, many Germans had worked in England, and some gave letters to be posted to friends or girlfriends they had hurriedly left in August. Several photographs were taken, showing groups of German and British troops huddling together, freezing cold but quite relaxed in each other's company.

Sometimes, meetings like these occurred when a truce had been arranged among the officers, to bury the dead left lying between the trenches. Here, burial parties stopped to talk to each other. In other parts of the Front, especially where opposing trenches were very close, soldiers simply called over, promising not to shoot their opponents if they would come out to meet them.

Over on the front line between Frelinghien and Houplines, Leutnant Johannes Niemann of the 133rd Royal Saxon Regiment faced the Scottish Seaforth Highlanders. His soldiers had boldly walked into the pockmarked land between the trenches to talk with their enemy. Now, to Niemann's astonishment, one of the Scottish soldiers had run up from his trench with a soccer ball. Then, within moments, two sets of goal posts were improvised with helmets on the frozen ground.

Niemann remembered the game clearly. Despite the language barrier, and the fact that these same men had been trying to kill each other only the day before, the game was remarkably good-natured. Both sides played with a fierce determination to win, but all kept quite rigorously to the rules, even without the advantage of a referee. The Germans were astonished to discover that these Scottish soldiers wore nothing under their kilts. Whenever a fierce tackle or a strong gust of wind revealed a Scotsman's buttocks, they would hoot and whistle like schoolboys.

The game went on for at least an hour, though soon enough word filtered back to the local German High Command. The senior officers there were strongly disapproving, and Niemann and the other junior officers were ordered to call their men back to their trenches immediately. "Still," Niemann later noted with some pride, "the game finished with a score of three goals to two in favour of Fritz against Tommy."

But not all the encounters were so friendly. Other matches were played with a marked animosity. A boxing match set up between two opposing regimental champions ended with the two men offering to finish each other off in a duel at one hundred paces.

In some parts of the Front, these strange meetings went on over the whole Christmas period. On December 30, one Yorkshire battalion received a message from their German counterparts warning them that they would have to start firing. The message explained, apologetically, that a German general was coming to inspect them that afternoon, and they had to put on a show of belligerence. When a British artillery battery was ordered to destroy a farmhouse just behind the German lines on January 1, they too sent word to the Germans warning them to leave the building.

Other Allied soldiers, such as the French and the Belgians, met their German counterparts too, but in far fewer numbers, and not with anything like the same cordiality. Perhaps the fact that the Germans were fighting from French or Belgian territory made the enmity between opponents more deeply felt and personal.

Field Marshal French's order of the day for Christmas Eve 1914, warning of a possible German attack, had been issued precisely because the Army High Command had feared that such contact with the enemy might occur. It had not been unusual, in earlier wars, for troops to fraternize with the enemy on Christmas Day. In the previous century, it was not unknown for opposing generals to sit down at Christmas dinner together.

The following December, after a year of dreary stalemate and occasional carnage, strict orders went out to both sides forbidding a repeat of the previous Christmas's goodwill.

"Nothing of the kind is to be allowed... this year. The artillery will maintain a slow gun fire on the enemy's trenches commencing at dawn, and every opportunity will be taken to inflict casualties upon any of the enemy exposing themselves," ran one order of the day to a British division.

Not everyone took notice of the order; but the fortunes of those who disobeyed were mixed. One officer in the Coldstream Guards, who went to shake hands with German soldiers who had come unarmed over No Man's Land, was sent home in disgrace. Other British troops, who had walked out to talk to their German opponents, were shelled by their own artillery. And, in most places, the open mixing of the previous year was successfully discouraged. One British officer noted with grim satisfaction that, when the Germans opposite started to sing carols, the British shelled them. Yet, even so, some troops still made friendly gestures to their enemies. On one part of the front line, opposing British and German soldiers lit fires in oil drums with pierced sides, and placed them along the tops of their trenches. "It was a wonderful sight," wrote one Scottish soldier. "I shall never forget it."

But, as the war dragged on, such old-fashioned civility became increasingly rare. As the casualty rate mounted, those who survived lost many of their friends and began to nurse increasingly bitter feelings about their enemy. By 1916 and 1917, such Christmas meetings had become extremely rare, although they did still occur in isolated parts of the

Front. By then, for most soldiers, a Christmas truce seemed as distant and unlikely as an end to the war itself. Even so, senior officers on both sides gave orders to step up artillery bombardments over the Christmas period, to ensure any such fraternization would never be repeated.

The great zeppelin campaign

1915-1918

On the night of May 31, 1915, the great dark shadow of German airship LZ-38 loomed above the clouds over London. The size of an ocean-going liner, it sailed through the sky at a steady 80kmph (50mph). Four powerful engines made such a deafening drone, conversation between Captain Erich Linnarz and his crew was almost impossible.

Through gaps in the clouds, the city could be seen clearly enough. Londoners were not expecting any kind of attack, and the lights of the West End streets and playhouses blazed brightly below. The capital's inhabitants felt perfectly safe. The Western Front was a reassuring distance away. And German warships, which sometimes attacked British coastal towns, lacked the range to hit this far inland.

Linnarz looked around, feeling rather pleased with himself. He later reported, "not a searchlight or anti-aircraft gun was aimed at us before the first bomb was dropped." He gave a curt nod to the bombardier close by in the control cabin, and 150 bombs rained down on the city below. Watching from their lofty perch, the crew could observe their bombs exploding. It was an exhilarating display. Fires broke out and buildings collapsed. In all, 42 people died or were seriously wounded that night – and worse was to come.

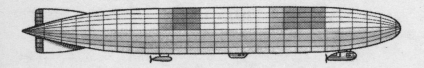

A German zeppelin of the First World War

The capital was visited by zeppelins, as the huge airships were known, throughout the summer. Named after their German inventor, Ferdinand Graf von Zeppelin, who had been flying these massive hydrogen-filled behemoths since 1897, they seemed to be the perfect weapon. Londoners grew to hate these sinister raiders. Although they did relatively little actual damage, the disruption and harm to morale they caused was formidable. Whenever a raid was on, traffic ground to a halt. People stared fearfully at the sky, and all electric lights were extinguished. When the bombs began to drop, people crouched in alleyways and cellars. They whispered in dread, in case their voices carried up to betray them. They were even afraid to strike a match to light a cigarette, in case the flare caught the attention of a zeppelin bombardier.

Despite its huge size, the zeppelin was almost invulnerable. Its main opponent, the fighter plane, could not fly high enough to attack it. Even when improvements in aircraft design allowed fighters to reach the altitude of a zeppelin, they still couldn't climb very quickly. So the invader would be long gone by the time the fighters got there. When the attacks began, 26 batteries of anti-aircraft (AA) guns were placed around London, and searchlights lit up the night sky with their bright, rapier beams. But these guns were also a new invention. The science of hitting flying machines, even ones as big as zeppelins, was complex. Hitting a moving target at that range, and priming a shell to explode at a particular height, were deadly arts yet to be perfected.

When war first broke out, the German kaiser, Wilhelm II, would not allow the zeppelins to be used over England. He was closely related to the British royal family, and he knew that bombing from the air would bring civilian casualties and severe family disapproval. But it soon became apparent that the war would not be over quickly; instead, it turned into a dreary stalemate with no end in sight, and the kaiser's own generals persuaded him it was his duty to use whatever advantage Germany might have.

So, in early January 1915, the first zeppelins appeared over the east coast of Britain, bringing massive disruption and anxiety. In this early stage of the war, the only threat zeppelin crews faced was the weather. Something so large and so ungainly was always going to be vulnerable to a strong wind.

Zeppelins crashed in storms; but nothing the enemy could throw at them had any effect.

These days, we have spy satellites and distant early warning (DEW) radar systems, to give us advanced warning, within seconds, of any potential enemy missile or bomber attack – even from the other side of the world. During the First World War, such technology had scarcely been imagined, let alone made available. Instead, the British had to rely on a network of human spotters placed along the coast – much as they had done for the arrival of the Spanish Armada during the time of Queen Elizabeth I. But the zeppelin spotters had at least the advantage of being able to report their sightings by telephone, rather than a chain of bonfires. They also used a cumbersome device called an orthophone – a huge, trumpet-like listening apparatus designed to detect the distant drone of the zeppelin's engines.

As the war dragged on, the design of fighter aircraft and AA guns raced forward. In 1914, flimsy planes could barely fly the English Channel. But, by 1916, the British had developed both aircraft and AA guns which were capable – at least in theory – of hitting the vast, slow-moving zeppelins. They also armed their aircraft with incendiary bullets, which were fired from machine guns mounted above the plane's cockpit. These projectiles, which glowed white-hot when discharged, were intended to set the highly flammable zeppelins alight. Zeppelin crews carried no parachutes – the available weight these huge machines could lift into the air was limited, and fuel and bombs were given priority over the crew's safety. Once a zeppelin caught fire, the crew had virtually no chance of escape. But such weapons were a great danger to the British pilots too, often exploding when used.

As zeppelin crews reported near-misses and lucky escapes from anti-aircraft fire on the ground, it was quickly decided that night attacks would be safer. As it turned out, they were also tremendously harmful. Curiously, it was the threat of attack, more than any actual damage done, which caused the most harm. If zeppelins were detected in the night sky, the order would be given to extinguish all lights below. This "blackout", as it became known, caused huge disruption and inconvenience, especially to factories and other local industries. But the blackout was also effective. Zeppelins sent out huge, powerful flares, hoping to find their way by briefly illuminating the land below. But launching such devices gave their position away to night fighter patrols and vigilant AA batteries.

As the zeppelins became more vulnerable to attack, they adopted more effective methods of defending themselves. Machine guns were mounted on top of their vast hulls. Manning them took special courage and stamina. A gunner would be tethered to his precarious position, exposed to both the machine guns of attacking fighter planes, and the freezing high-altitude temperatures and air currents. If he was injured or overcome by either, rescue was impossible.

One ingenious device employed to protect a zeppelin crew was the cloud car. Shaped like a fairground rocket ride, the car and its single passenger would be lowered from the interior of the zeppelin by a long cable that could dangle its load 800m (half a mile) below. The idea was that the zeppelin would lurk inside thick cloud, safely concealed from air and AA attack, while the cloud car dangled in the clear air beneath, too small to be seen in the vastness of the sky. Its passenger, in communication with the zeppelin via a telephone line, would then direct the ship towards its target. It was a hair-raisingly dangerous job. One cloud-car passenger was dashed to death on a cliff when his zeppelin flew too low over the coast. If the cable jammed or snapped, the cloud-car passenger was totally at the mercy of any enemy warplane that might spot him, and he could also be hit by bombs dropped from his own zeppelin. Yet, despite these additional dangers, there was no shortage of volunteers for cloud-car duty. Astonishingly, this was mainly because its passenger was allowed to smoke – an activity expressly forbidden in the zeppelin itself, with its highly inflammable, hydrogen-packaged fuselage.

For almost two years, the zeppelins were able to roam at will over Britain, their greatest foes the weather and their own occasional structural failures.

But on September 2, 1916, everything changed. That evening, the crew of German airship SL-11 and Lieutenant William Leefe Robinson, a pilot of 39 Squadron of the Home Defence Wing, Royal Flying Corps, were about to earn their place in history.

As the wet and dreary day drew to a close, 16 airships from the German navy and army services took to the air and began their long journey through the darkening skies over the North Sea. This was the largest fleet of airships so far assembled by the Germans, and their target was to be the British military headquarters in London.

Not all were zeppelins. Half of the fleet had been manufactured by the rival airship firm Schütte-Lanz, who made their flying machines with wooden, rather than light metal, frames. For the British, however, such differences were academic – the Schütte-Lanz airships were equally formidable. SL-11, for example, was 174m (570ft) long and 21m (70ft) high, and could carry a similar number of bombs.

Robinson and his fellow pilots had a new anti-zeppelin weapon in their arsenal; although it was one they had very little confidence in. The British had been using incendiary bullets against airships for as long as they had been trying to shoot them down. However, to date, these bullets had proved ineffective. New, more powerful incendiaries had been developed, but so far the results had been disastrous. The new type of bullet was prone to explode in the weapon firing it, and almost 20 British warplanes had been destroyed trying to use it.

As night fell, radio operators at listening stations picked up a noticeable increase in German wireless communications, suggesting a massive raid was in progress. Spotters along the coast were informed, and began to scan the skies for any incoming airships.

By ten o'clock that evening, the airship fleet had been detected as it approached the Norfolk coast. The massive sound of its combined engines hinted at the size of the attack. London AA gun batteries and airfields were alerted. Over on Sutton's Farm airfield, 30km (20 miles) southwest of London, Lieutenant Robinson prepared his BE2 biplane for takeoff.

A BE2 biplane

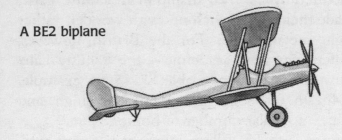

These lumbering two-seater planes were normally used as reconnaissance aircraft, but their wide wings and powerful engines enabled them to fly higher than many of the faster, more agile fighters in the Royal Flying Corps. As the BE2s earmarked to intercept zeppelins usually only carried one crew member, rather than two, the lack of extra weight helped the plane climb higher still. Robinson headed off into the moonless sky just after half past eleven.

That night, he would be one of six pilots out to try their luck in the dangerous skies over the capital.

These days, flying at over 1.5km (1 mile) every three seconds, modern jet fighters can reach high altitudes in a matter of minutes. In 1916, it took an entire hour for Robinson's BE2 to reach 3,000m (10,000 ft). Peering through the velvet sky, hoping to spot a looming black hull, he could see nothing. He even switched off his engine, in the hope of hearing the approaching airships.

Just after one in the morning, while flying over the docks at Gravesend, Robinson spotted a zeppelin, the LZ-98. Turning in to attack, he unleashed a hail of bullets into the vast body of the airship. Nothing happened – except that, as soon as the crew realized they were being attacked, they executed a standard zeppelin procedure. The LZ-98 rose swiftly in the air, way out of reach of the BE2. But just as Robinson gave up and turned away, he caught sight of something else lurking in the clouds below. A searchlight had illuminated another airship.

It was the SL-11, returning home after dropping its bombs on the northern suburbs of the capital. Half an hour earlier, the airship had been the focus of most of the anti-aircraft guns of north and central London. They had failed; but the volume of fire bursting around the SL-11 had convinced its captain, Hauptmann Wilhelm Schramm, to turn his giant ship around and head further north.

As Robinson wheeled in to face his enemy, the SL-11 vanished into a bank of clouds. Twenty minutes passed. Then, just when he was contemplating returning home before his fuel ran out, Robinson spotted the airship again. AA guns were firing up at it, and searchlights occasionally caught the huge hull in their beam.

He turned his BE2 to face the shadow. This time, he was determined not to let his quarry slip away. But, just as he was preparing to fire his machine gun, his plane rocked alarmingly, buffeted by an explosion just underneath him. The AA guns below were also firing up at the airship – and exploding at the height they guessed their target was flying. They had no idea a British plane was up there too. In those days, pilots did not have radios to alert their comrades below, but the Royal Flying Corps did have a procedure for such emergencies. The pilot could fire off a flare to let the AA gunners know he was up there. But Robinson knew this would also warn the airship crew that he was stalking them. So he pressed on, hoping his own plane would not be hit.

The BE2 approached its target from below, swooping over to the front of the hull. Then, as the vast shadow loomed over him, Robinson began to fire his incendiary bullets into the great, gas-filled body of the ship. His highly detailed account of the attack makes for a vivid read:

"I made nose down in the direction of the

zeppelin. I saw shells bursting and night tracer shells flying around it. When I drew closer I noticed that the anti-aircraft aim was too high or too low; also a good many some 800ft [240m] behind... I flew along about 800ft below it from bow to stern and distributed one drum [of ammunition] along it. It seemed to have no effect."

As he began placing a fresh magazine on his machine gun – a tricky process, as he had to fly at the same time – the airship machine gunners opened up. He weaved away into the black night, then headed in for a second attempt. Firing all along the side of the airship, he emptied his entire ammunition drum; and still nothing happened.

On that run, he flew so close to the crew control car, he could see the silhouettes of men inside. Perhaps they were not aware he was attacking them. After all, they were engrossed in their bombing of the territory below, and the roar of their own engines would have prevented them from hearing his tiny plane. By now, Robinson was beginning to feel angry. The incendiaries obviously posed far more danger to the pilot firing them than to the airship they were aimed at. But, risking attack from the guns of both the Germans and his own side, he flew in for a third time, as close as he dared:

"I then got close behind it (by this time I was very close – 500ft [150m] or less below) and concentrated one drum on one part (underneath rear)... I had hardly finished the drum before I saw the part fired at glow. When the third drum was fired there were no searchlights on the zeppelin and no anti-aircraft was firing. I quickly got out of the way of the falling zeppelin and being very excited fired off a few red Very lights★ and dropped a parachute flare."

Something awesome had happened inside the body of the airship. The gas bag where he had concentrated his fire had ignited, lighting up the inside of the hull like a magic lantern. Then the stern of the airship burst open in an immense explosion, which tossed his tiny plane like a paper dart in a gale. The fire quickly spread along the entire body of the ship. Once he had regained control of his plane, Robinson could see many of the crew throwing themselves out of the zeppelin, to avoid being burned to death.

He let off his flares because he was determined the AA gunners below should know it was he who had downed the airship and not them. As he turned his plane to return to the airbase, he noted that the SL-11 had crashed into the ground. So bright was the blazing hull that he could make out the shapes of houses all along the outer rim of northeast London.

Robinson had proved it *was* possible to down these huge machines. Despite the early hour, all over London people rushed out into the streets to sing and dance. Church bells rang, sirens wailed, and ships'

★Very lights were bright flares, fired from a specially adapted pistol.

horns and motor horns tooted. The airships had caused such dread, for so long; but now it seemed there was a way of hitting back at them.

For the German airship crews still approaching the city over the flatlands of Suffolk and Cambridgeshire that night, the huge blaze lighting up the sky in the far distance was an ominous sight. Their airships were not indestructible after all. Perhaps the demise of SL-11 affected their performance, because the raid on London that night was not a success. Although the 16 airships dropped a huge number of bombs between them, only four people were killed and another 12 injured. Damage to buildings was put at £21,072. In comparison, 16 trained airmen aboard SL-11 had lost their lives, and their £94,000 airship had been destroyed.

SL-11 fell to earth behind the Plough Inn pub, by the village of Cuffley, Hertfordshire. The next day, the village was besieged by sightseers, and the country lanes nearby were clogged with cars, carts, bicycles and pedestrians. The burned-out frame of tangled steel and wire, with the broken gondolas and smashed engines, was a startling sight. To the side of the wreckage, a green tarpaulin was laid on the ground to hide the charred remains of those members of the crew who had not leaped to their deaths. Other bodies would be found in the next few days, scattered over the countryside on SL-11's last, doomed flight path.

Robinson's method of attack — a sustained burst of

incendiary fire at one concentrated spot – was immediately passed on to all fighter pilots likely to encounter a German airship. Such daring deserved reward. Robinson was presented with the Victoria Cross – the highest award for bravery that can be given to members of the British armed forces. But thereafter, the fortunes of this 21-year-old fighter pilot declined. He was shot down over German-occupied France eight months later, and spent the rest of the war in a prison camp, where he was badly treated because he had shot down the SL-11. At the end of the war, he became one of many millions of victims of a massive flu epidemic that swept through the world, and died on New Year's Eve, 1918.

Robinson's victory had an impact far beyond the simple destruction of one airship. The swaggering confidence that airship crews had displayed in their mess halls and barracks was gone. Nights away from flying duty were haunted by dreams of burning airships. Now, they were no longer invulnerable, like the gods of ancient Greece or Rome, casting death and destruction down from the skies. They too were flesh and blood. When death came, as it did with increasing regularity, the entire crew would perish.

From then on, the zeppelin raids grew less frequent and more costly. From the spring of 1917, German Gotha bombers were sent over London instead. They were faster, flew higher, and could defend themselves from fighter planes more effectively. Yet the Germans still nursed high hopes for their magnificent airships. By the end of the war, the latest model zeppelins were even earmarked for a raid on New York. Luckily for the Americans, the war ended before such an attack could be mounted.

The Battle of Jutland

May-June 1916

In late May 1916, anyone climbing the heathery hills of Hoy in the Scottish Orkney Islands could have peered through the mist of the vast Scapa Flow inlet and seen one of the most magnificent sights in naval history. For here was the home of the British Grand Fleet. Almost as far as the eye could see sat row upon row of battleships, battlecruisers, cruisers, destroyers – and scores of lesser vessels scurrying between these deadly ships with supplies, men and messages. Each ship was spaced at a neat interval and at exactly the same angle to every other – a visible representation of the discipline and tradition of this most prestigious fighting force. And, astonishingly, the power of the British navy did not end with this vast collection of ships. There were other bases too, at Cromarty, Moray Firth and Rosyth, along the eastern coast of Scotland. Each contained a formidable battle squadron of warships, all under the command of Admiral John Jellicoe.

At the time of the First World War, Britain had the greatest fleet in the world. They needed it too. Island Britain had an empire that stretched from the Arctic to Antarctic Circles. Their warships protected the fleets of cargo ships which carried goods and raw materials to and from British colonies. During wartime, the warships also prevented cargo ships from delivering goods to Britain's enemies. Most crucial of all, the British fleet ensured that supplies and troops from England could sail safely across the Channel to the Western Front in northern France. Only Germany had a fleet powerful enough to threaten the British. As the head of state of an up-and-coming superpower, Kaiser Wilhelm II had wanted to build a rival navy to complement Germany's growing importance in the world. But Wilhelm's policy was a double-edged sword. His insistence on building a powerful navy had soured previously good Anglo-German relations, and had been one of the main reasons Britain joined France and Russia against Germany when war broke out.

Today, it is difficult to imagine the hold battleships had on the imagination of people at the start of the 20th century. In the early 21st century, such weapons are largely obsolete; aircraft carriers, warplanes with their formidable arsenal of bombs and missiles, and the intangible threat of terrorism are the stuff of modern warfare. But, at the start of the First World War, the battleship was considered the superweapon of its day. The largest and most heavily armed battleships were known as dreadnoughts – after *HMS Dreadnought*, the first of their kind, launched in 1906.

Dreadnought weighed a formidable 17,900 tons and packed a mighty punch with ten 12-inch★ (30cm) guns. By the time war broke out many of these dreadnought battleships had even bigger guns — 13.5-inch (34cm) monsters, that could fire a shell weighing 640kg (1,400lb) over 21km (13 miles). These guns were housed in pairs in large turrets, usually at the front and rear of the ship. Such weaponry gave the battleship its ferocious bite. Each gun turret had a crew of around 70 men, split into teams who performed the complex task of bringing up shells and propulsive charges from the ship's magazine, and then loading, aiming and accurately dispatching them. Working in such a turret could be exceptionally dangerous. If an enemy shell hit the turret, the entire mechanism would be engulfed in a massive explosion, killing everyone inside it.

HMS Dreadnought overshadowed every other warship afloat. Not only was it very powerfully armed, it was fast and shielded by a thick metal protective covering. This ship carried a crew of over a thousand men, and was nearly 215m (700ft) from bow (front) to stern (rear). The arrival of *HMS Dreadnought* began a ruinously expensive arms race between Britain and Germany. By the time war broke out, Britain had built 28 such ships, and Germany 16.

The revolutionary dreadnoughts were also joined by another new kind of warship, the battlecruiser. The first of their kind was *HMS Invincible*, launched

52 ★ The guns on warships were referred to by the width (in inches) of the shells they fired. A 12-inch gun fired a shell that was 12 inches wide.

in April 1907. Battlecruisers were smaller but almost as heavily armed as dreadnoughts, with eight 12-inch (30cm) guns. They were faster than battleships, having a top speed of around 25 knots, compared to a battleship's 21. But this speed was gained at the expense of lighter protection.

When war began in August 1914, a full-scale confrontation between the British and German fleets seemed inevitable – in fact, both countries had built up their massive navies to face such a task. The German fleet may have been smaller than the British fleet, but its ships were better designed. The Germans also made very effective use of their U-boats, sinking so many cargo ships bound for Britain that the country was often in danger of starvation. But, throughout the war, the British never lost control of the sea. The Royal Navy placed a blockade around German waters, preventing vital goods from getting in. This caused great difficulty for Germany's war industries, and ensured that there was never enough food for her home population.

Barely six months into the war, the German battlecruiser *Blücher* was sunk in the North Sea, with great loss of life. The disaster led to the sacking of the German navy commander-in-chief, Admiral Ingenohl. But it also encouraged his successor, Admiral Hugo von Pohl, to be extremely cautious. Then, in February 1916, suffering from ill health, von Pohl resigned. He was replaced by Admiral Reinhard

Scheer, a far more aggressive and daring commander-in-chief.

For the first two years of the war, each navy had tested the strength of its opponents, tentatively pushing and probing, engaging in small-scale skirmishes, with only the occasional battle. But, as the carnage of the Western Front continued with no visible benefit to either side, pressure mounted on the German navy's High Command to force the British into a do-or-die battle that could tip the balance of the war Germany's way.

Scheer decided that the German fleet would try to lure the British into the North Sea for a grand confrontation. Today, such a move would be called a "high-risk strategy". If Scheer succeeded, the war would be as good as won. With its fleet destroyed, Britain would be unable to prevent a German naval blockade around her coastal waters. Food supplies would quickly run out, and the country would starve. British troops and supplies would no longer be able to travel safely across the Channel. The great British politician Winston Churchill once described Admiral Jellicoe as the only man who could lose the war in an afternoon. In the early summer of 1916, Jellicoe had the chance to do just that.

Scheer's plan was simple enough. He would send a battlecruiser squadron into the North Sea, under the command of Admiral Franz von Hipper. Then he would follow at a distance with his High Seas Fleet.

The British, it was hoped, would send out their own battlecruisers to intercept Hipper's ships. These would almost certainly come from the base at Rosyth, which was the nearest to the outgoing German ships. When the British were sighted on the horizon, Hipper would change course, and lead the enemy back to Scheer's main battle fleet. Here, outnumbered, they would be destroyed.

The plan also assumed that the main British naval force – the aptly named Grand Fleet – would take to sea too, from the more northerly base of Scapa Flow. Here, Scheer meant for lurking U-boats to pick them off as they sailed to intercept him; and he intended to use zeppelins to keep watch on the British navy and radio in information on the movements of their ships.

But, like many simple plans, there were unforeseen hitches...

On May 31, 1916, Scheer put his plan in motion. From bases on the northern coast of Germany, the High Seas Fleet took to sea. Admiral von Hipper set out ahead with five battlecruisers and another 35 smaller ships, to try to lure the British navy into battle. Scheer followed on, in the battleship *Friedrich der Grosse*, accompanied by 60 other battleships, battlecruisers, cruisers and destroyers, and sundry smaller boats. By one o'clock that afternoon, the two German squadrons were way out in the North Sea, 80km (50 miles) apart.

As they had intended, von Hipper's squadron was soon sighted by the British reconnaissance ships that patrolled the coast off Germany. British intelligence had also picked up and decoded German radio signals which indicated that there was a build up of German ships in the North Sea. As foreseen by Scheer, Admiral Jellicoe immediately ordered his Rosyth battlecruiser squadron, under Admiral Beatty, to take to sea. But, unknown to Sheer, Jellicoe was already at sea with his Grand Fleet, patrolling an area of the North Sea known as the "Long Forties", 180km (110 miles) east of Aberdeen. Jellicoe ordered the Grand Fleet to head south and follow Beatty. Between them, the two British admirals had 149 ships under their command.

The stage was set for an epic confrontation. To this day, no greater naval battle has ever taken place. The opposing admirals, perched high in command posts above the decks of their ships, began a game that was a strange combination of hide-and-seek and chess. At stake were the lives of 100,000 sailors, the fate of nearly 250 ships and, quite possibly, the outcome of the First World War. Jellicoe, particularly, was hoping for a victory to match Trafalgar. There, in 1805, the Royal Navy under Admiral Nelson had destroyed the French and Spanish fleets, and left Britain in undisputed control of the sea for the next century.

Right from the start, Scheer's scheme did not go to plan. The U-boats stationed outside the bases on the Scottish coast failed to attack the British ships as they emerged to patrol the North Sea. A technical problem meant that wireless orders permitting them to engage their enemy were never received.

Scheer's novel use of zeppelins as reconnaissance aircraft was also a failure, due to bad weather and poor visibility. The zeppelins could see almost nothing through cloud or foggy haze. This was a major drawback. Today, thanks to radar and satellite surveillance, navy commanders can detect an approaching enemy long before his ships or aircraft are even over the horizon. In 1916, navy ships and guns were immeasurably more sophisticated and powerful than those used by Nelson at Trafalgar; but their communication and detection technology was much the same. Scheer and Jellicoe might have had guns which could fire a heavy shell 22km (14 miles), but they still looked for their enemy with a telescope and naked eye. Also, due to the danger of wireless communications being intercepted by the enemy, in battle they still preferred to communicate with their ships using signal flags and semaphore.*

Early that afternoon, neither admiral knew the size of the enemy fleet fast approaching them. The British thought only Hipper's squadron was at sea. And Scheer had no idea he was soon to face the entire Grand Fleet.

Beatty's fleet first sighted von Hipper's ships at around two o'clock, when they were about 121km

*A method of ship-to-ship communication whereby particular hand positions, indicated by a sailor carrying two flags, stand for letters of the alphabet.

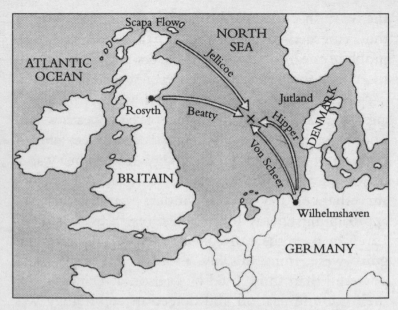

The Battle of Jutland

(75 miles) off the Danish coast of Jutland. Thereafter, the epic confrontation that followed would be known as the Battle of Jutland.

The first shots were fired about 15 minutes later, between small scout ships, which sailed ahead of the main fleets. The day was quite hazy, and the sun was now well behind the German ships, giving them a much better view of their approaching enemy.

Beatty sailed forward to engage von Hipper's forces. By then, it was around half past three. Beatty knew the Grand Fleet was coming up behind him, but he would be on his own for several crucial hours before Jellicoe caught up with him. Hipper, in turn, knew he had to lure Beatty's ships into the jaws of the High Seas fleet behind him. As they had done in the days of Nelson and Trafalgar, both fleets sailed "in line" – that is, one after the other, in tight formation.

At ten to four, the battlecruisers began firing at each other. The odds seemed to be on Beatty's side. He had six battlecruisers, where Hipper had five. Almost immediately, firing between the opposing forces was so constant that each squadron seemed to be navigating its way through a thick forest of towering shell splashes. Bizarrely, in the No Man's Land between the fleets, a small sailing boat sat motionless. Its sails hung limp in the still air as deadly shells whistled and screamed, arcing high over the heads of the hapless sailors on board.

The superiority of the German guns and ships soon became obvious. Just after four o'clock, just 12 minutes into the fighting, the British battlecruiser *Indefatigable* became the first major casualty of the day. The German ship *Von Der Tann* had landed three shells on her almost simultaneously. *Indefatigable* disappeared in a vast cloud of black smoke, twice the height of her mast, and fell out of line, as she was hit by two more shells from *Von Der Tann*. Inside *Indefatigable* something terrible was happening. Searing flames were gnawing at her ammunition supplies. Thirty seconds after the second shells hit home, the entire ship exploded, sending huge fragments of metal high into the air. She rolled over

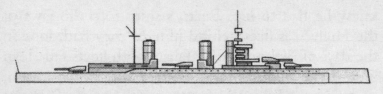

Beatty's battlecruiser, the *Lion* (213m/700ft long)

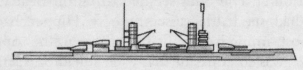

Scheer's battleship, the *Friedrich der Grosse* (172m/566ft long)

and sank moments later. Only two men on board survived, rescued by a German torpedo boat.

Among several other British ships, Beatty's own battlecruiser *Lion* was hit, when a shell penetrated the central turret, blowing half the roof into the air and killing the entire gun crew. The roar of the guns, and the whistle of the shells as they approached, was enough to distract anyone from what was happening to other ships around them. Aboard the *Lion*, Beatty barely noticed the loss of *Indefatigable*. He had enough troubles of his own. Six shells from von Hipper's flagship, the battlecruiser *Lützow*, hit his ship within four minutes, and fires raged on deck and below. Half an hour later, another explosion caused by slow-burning fires shot up as high as the masthead. But the *Lion*, and Beatty, survived to fight on.

The other British ships fighting alongside had to contend with similar problems. Twenty minutes later, the battlecruiser *Queen Mary* blew up too, breaking in half and sinking within 90 seconds. When the ammunition supplies exploded, the huge gun-turret roofs were blown 30m (100 feet) into the air. Only eight men survived from the entire ship. One of them was gunner Ernest Francis.

When the *Queen Mary* began to sink, he called out to his comrades around him: "Come on you chaps, who's coming for a swim?"

Someone replied, "She'll float for a long time yet."

But Francis knew in his bones he had to get away. Diving into the freezing, oily water, he began to swim as fast as he could away from his ship. Within a minute there was a huge explosion, and chunks of metal filled the air around him. Only diving deep beneath the waves saved him from being killed by flying fragments. When he reached the surface, gasping for breath, he was immediately dragged under again by the downward suction of the ship as it sank. Beneath the water, he felt utterly helpless and resigned to death.

"What's the use of your struggling?" he said to himself. "You're done."

But something made him strike out for the surface. Just as he was about to lose consciousness, he broke through the waves. Ahead was a piece of floating debris, and Francis wrapped his wrist around a rope trailing from it before he became unconscious. Eventually he was rescued, but not before an earlier ship had picked up the few other survivors, leaving him for dead.

Beatty had seen the destruction of the *Queen Mary* at close hand. In the strange and rather callous manner of the British upper class at war, he remarked on the loss of the *Queen Mary* and *Indefatigable*, and over 2,000 lives: "There seems to be something wrong with our bloody ships today."

There *was* something wrong with the British ships: they were badly designed. German warships had solid bulkheads (the partitions inside a vessel), passable only by going to the upper deck and then down into the next section. British ships had bulkheads with doors that permitted passage between them. This was far more convenient, of course, but a serious weakness when a massive explosion ripped through a ship. The British also had a much more careless attitude to their ammunition. German shells were kept locked away in blast-proof containers until they were ready to be fired. British gunners piled their shells next to their guns. So they were far easier to set off accidentally if the ship was hit.

But Beatty's *sang froid* in the midst of the partial destruction of his own ship was admirable too. Unlike army generals who direct land battles from headquarters behind the front line, when fighting starts at sea, an admiral has just as much chance of being killed by an enemy shell as the most humble seaman.

Moments after the *Queen Mary* sank, Scheer's German High Seas Fleet was spotted steaming over the horizon to join von Hipper's battlecruiser squadron. Jellicoe and his Grand Fleet were still 20km (12 miles) away. Beatty's composure was being tested to the limit. Facing both Scheer's and Hipper's forces, and two battlecruisers down, Beatty gave the signal for a 180° turn. Scheer's plan, to use Hipper's forces to entice the British into the jaws of the High Seas Fleet, was now being turned on its head. As the German ships pursued the fleeing British, Beatty was now luring them into the massed fire power of the British Grand Fleet.

Shortly after five o'clock that afternoon, Scheer's fleet had come close enough to Beatty's retreating ships to begin attacking the stragglers. But, an hour later, Jellicoe's fleet of 24 battleships was steaming over the horizon. No matter how good the German ships were, they were now heavily outnumbered. Scheer was in serious trouble, and he sent out an order for his ships to head north.

Jellicoe was puzzled. From his position high on his flagship *Iron Duke*, he could observe the enemy turning away from him; but he was suspicious. Was Scheer trying to lead them into a trap, hoping perhaps that the British would blunder into a minefield, or into the path of waiting submarines? There was too much at stake. So Jellicoe decided not to follow. Instead, his ships were ordered to head south, where Jellicoe guessed they might once again make contact with the German fleet.

Meanwhile, von Hipper's ship *Lützow* had been badly damaged and he was forced to abandon her, transferring to the battlecruiser *Seydlitz*, and then to the *Moltke*. But the *Lützow* still managed to sink another British ship. The unlucky vessel was the very first battlecruiser, *Invincible* – the third major victim of the day. At half past six, a shell hit one of her gun turrets, causing a huge explosion which broke the ship in two. Of the 1,032 men on board, only six survived. For a while, both the bow and stern of this huge, 17,000-ton battlecruiser stood motionless in the water, like two church spires in a sunken village. Then the stern began a relentless descent to the bottom of the sea. The bow stayed upright until the next day, when it too sank. Those trapped inside must have spent an agonizing night, wondering what on earth was happening to them in their topsy-turvy world. Expecting to be swallowed by the sea when the ship went vertical in the water, their inevitable death was drawn out for a miserable few hours more.

As the evening wore on, Jellicoe's intuition that the German ships would head south proved correct. Soon after seven, the two fleets sighted each other again. Scheer made several moves to try to place his fleet at an advantage to the British. Both sides were following a tactic known as "crossing the T". The idea was to line up your fleet of warships at a right angle to your opponent's, as they approached you in a straight line, so your fleet made the top of the "T" and the enemy fleet made the descending stroke. In that way, a commander could fire all the guns aboard his ships, both bow and stern, while his enemy would only be able to use his front guns.

But Scheer failed to outwit his enemy and, disastrously, found his ships scattered at an angle to the approaching British fleet. Worse still, the sun was now behind the British, and it was only possible to see them by the flash of their guns. At this point in the battle it was British shells that were falling with greater accuracy, while Scheer's ships were faltering.

It was at this moment that Scheer made the most ruthless decision of the day. To avoid his entire fleet being reduced to wreckage by the much larger British force, Scheer ordered Admiral Hipper to take his squadron of four battlecruisers and sail straight at the British fleet. His signal read: "Battlecruisers at the enemy! Give it everything!" There was a cruel logic to his decision. Hipper's fleet was made up of older and less powerful warships; Scheer would be saving his best ships to fight another day. This action has subsequently become known as the "death ride". Scheer intended the British fleet to concentrate their fire on von Hipper's force, allowing the rest of his High Seas Fleet to turn away and escape.

Von Hipper's ships – *Derfflinger*, *Seydlitz*, *Moltke* and *Von der Tann* – had been in the thick of the action since the battle began. All had sustained serious damage. As they headed out into the fading light, each ship's captain was convinced he would not live to see the coming night. But, in warfare, nothing is predictable.

Ahead of them, Beatty and Jellicoe's ships seemed to stretch in a curve as far as they could see. Every one of these British ships began to fire directly on the four approaching German battlecruisers. Leading these warships was the *Derfflinger*. Its chief gunnery officer, Georg von Hase, recorded:

> "[We] now came under a particularly deadly fire... steaming at full speed into this inferno, offering a splendid target to the enemy while they were still hard to make out... Salvo after salvo fell around us, hit after hit struck our ship."

Both the main rear turrets of the *Derfflinger* suffered direct hits, exploding with horrific consequences for those inside. But, thanks to good design, the rest of the ship survived. The other German battlecruisers suffered similar blows but, although they took many hits from British shells, these formidable ships were not blown to pieces.

Von Hipper was a brave commander, but he had no intention of committing suicide. Once he was sure the rest of the German fleet had escaped, his ships turned away to rejoin the rear of Scheer's departing squadrons. Again Jellicoe was suspicious. Rather than following von Hipper's ships directly, he turned south and raced to catch them via a more indirect route. Just as the sun was sinking on the horizon, von Hipper's slower squadron was caught again by the British. This time, they were not so lucky. *Lützow* sustained more damage and would sink later that night, and *Seydlitz* and *Derfflinger* were badly damaged.

In the dark the two opposing navies continued to exchange fire, but the main action was over. The German battleship *Pommern* was one of the final victims of the battle. Four torpedoes from British destroyers caught her close to home, and all 866 men on board were killed.

Dawn broke around three o'clock on the morning of June 1. Jellicoe had hoped to resume contact with the German fleet at first light, but his lookouts strained their eyes over an empty sea. The German ships were in sight of their home port, and the battle was over.

The two greatest navies in the world had taken part in the one great sea battle of the First World War. In fact, it was to be the last great sea battle in history. Thereafter, battleships would never again meet in such numbers. As the century wore on, there would be naval weapons even deadlier than the great guns that battleships carried – insidious submarines, phalanxes of dive bombers and, more recently, fast and accurate guided missiles. All of these technological advances made battleships too vulnerable to be useful weapons.

Scheer's gamble had failed, but the events of the day had shown that he had had every right to be confident. Germany's ships were better than Britain's, and they had proved this by sinking more of their enemy's fleet. The British lost 14 ships and 6,274 men; the Germans, 11 ships and 1,545 men. On the day after the battle, it looked like a German victory. But, in the end, the might of the Royal Navy had prevailed. Britain still controlled the sea. Like the other grand battles of 1916 at Verdun and the Somme, a clash of huge opposing forces had taken place, and nothing had changed. Jellicoe had not lost the war in an afternoon after all. He hadn't won it either; but he *had* ensured that Germany would not win it.

After the battle, the tactics employed by Jellicoe and Beatty were dissected and discussed in clinical detail. Communication between the British ships had been very poor and Jellicoe, in particular, was criticized for not attacking the German fleet with more enthusiasm. But, with hindsight, the British still came out of it less badly than the Germans. It only took them a day to recover from the battle, before Jellicoe was able to announce that his fleet was once again ready for whatever threat it might face. The German High Seas Fleet, on the other hand, never put to sea again.

The outcome of the battle of Jutland had far-reaching consequences. As the High Seas Fleet had proved unable to undermine British control of the seas, the German High Command decided to adopt a policy of unrestricted U–boat warfare instead. This meant their submarines were given permission to attack any ship, including neutral ones, that they came across in British waters. This change of tactics led to the sinking of American ships, which in turn became one of the main reasons the United States entered the war against Germany – a move which assured her defeat.

The great German High Seas Fleet remained in port for the rest of the war. Boredom and poor rations led to mutinies and, at the end of the war, revolutionary insurrection. After the armistice of November 1918, the fleet was ordered to sail to Scapa Flow while peace terms were discussed in Paris. Shortly before the peace treaty was signed in the summer of 1919, it was suggested that the High Seas Fleet should be split up and its ships given to the victorious nations. But this was too much to bear for the skeleton crews of German sailors left aboard the ships, and so they scuttled - deliberately sank - their navy in Scapa Flow. Eventually, most of these vast, magnificent warships were raised from the sea bottom and towed away for scrap. But some still remain to this day, where they are a constant source of fascination for divers.

The first day of
the Somme

July 1, 1916

Moving images were first captured on film in the
early 1890s. By the time the First World War broke
out in 1914, movie cameras were an accustomed
sight at any momentous event. Although the war is
best remembered through photographs, much of it
was also captured on black and white movie film.
There are dramatic shots of artillery bombardments
and full-scale infantry attacks, and chilling footage of
the aftermath of close-quarter trench fighting. But
one of the most haunting scenes of the war to be
caught on film was not very spectacular at all. It
shows a platoon of British soldiers resting before they
"go over the top" on the morning of Saturday July 1,
1916 – the first day of the Battle of the Somme.

The time is about 7:25am, five minutes before the
start of the attack. Filmed in a sunken road on the
edge of the British front line, the men stare uneasily
into the camera, faces tense with anxiety. They had
been assured by their commanders that the
forthcoming battle would be a walkover, but few, it
seemed, believed this. Some share a final cigarette,
one or two crack grim jokes, their mouths smiling or

laughing, but their eyes full of fear. They all look immaculate – freshly shaven and well turned-out. For many, it would be their first time in battle. For most, it would be the last five or ten minutes of their lives. In the final moments before battle, they fix their bayonets to the ends of their rifles, and then they are gone. Within a few minutes, most were killed – caught out in the open by murderously effective machine-gun fire from the German trenches.

For a great number of the men embroiled in the Somme offensive, their journey to oblivion began in the first days following the outbreak of war. The soldiers who took part in this great battle were mainly volunteers who had joined up at the beginning. They had been dubbed "Kitchener's Army", after the British war secretary, Lord Kitchener, who had appeared on recruitment posters asking for volunteers.

A million men flocked to join – many enticed by the promise that they could serve alongside their friends in what became known as "Pals battalions". The idea was a good one in theory. Battalions within a regiment would be made up of men from the same town, or village, or workplace. They trained and worked together; and when the time came, they would fight together too.

The smoky, industrial town of Accrington, Lancashire, was one such community. It provided a "Pals" battalion for the East Lancashire Regiment.

When war broke out, the town had hit hard times. A strike at the local textile machinery factory had ended in stalemate. A local cotton mill had also laid off 500 men and women. Undoubtedly, many men rushed to join up for the benefit of a soldier's pay as much as for any patriotic motive. The pay was, after all, twice what workers got in the mill or factory. Those not tempted by financial advantage faced more subtle pressures. One recruitment poster declared: "Will you fight for your King and Country, or will you skulk in the safety your fathers won and your brothers are struggling to maintain?" Another poster carried a more personal message, with a young man being shamed by his girlfriend's father: "Look here... if you're old enough to walk out with my daughter, you are old enough to fight for her and your Country."

Whatever these other reasons for joining, many men also did so out of plain, honest patriotism – an unquestioning feeling of duty and love of country. Accrington was a poor town, and a good number of those who flocked to enlist were malnourished and small in stature. Many failed their medical examination and were rejected as recruits, much to their disappointment and even humiliation. But such was the outcry in the region, these standards were dropped. Instead of requiring recruits who were at least 18, over 5ft 6in (168cm) tall and with a chest measurement of 35in (89cm), the rules were relaxed to 5ft 3in tall and 34in in the chest. Age was never a problem, as it was easy enough for 16 year olds to pass themselves off as older; and this was rarely checked. Local worthies, who had huffed and puffed that the army top brass in London had "dared to think Lancashire patriotism could be measured in inches", were mollified.

When it was time to go, the new recruits lined up in the market square and marched down to the grimy granite railway station, watched by the whole town. They milled onto overcrowded platforms and waited for the steam train that would whisk them away from their familiar world. Seeing photographs of these men smiling bravely for the camera, their lower legs wrapped in puttees (tightly woven khaki cotton bands, which was part of the uniform at the time), it is plain that they had no idea what they were letting themselves in for.

As 1915 drew to a close, the British and French high commands became convinced that the way to end the war would be one "big push" – a massive attack, on a broad front, that would be enough to break the German lines and form a gap for the cavalry to rush through. Such a tactic, if successful, would reinstate a "war of movement", instead of the dreadful stalemate of the trenches. The spot chosen for the big push was the Somme, a chalky part of northern France near the Belgian border, named after the river that runs through it. The Somme had no particular strategic value. It was picked merely because this was the area of the Western Front where the British and French lines met – the most convenient spot for a combined attack.

But, as the new year began, the Germans had their own plans. Intending to "bleed the French army white", wearing them down by constant attack, the German chief-of-staff, General von Falkenhayn, launched a dreadful battle of attrition on the French fortress of Verdun. Beginning in February 1916, Falkenhayn succeeded all too well, though at dreadful cost to his own army. The French army never really recovered from Verdun, and was certainly in no position to offer more than token support to the British when their own big push began in the summer.

In these circumstances, British commander-in-chief, Field Marshal Haig, and the Fourth Army commander, General Rawlinson, who commanded British troops in that section of the Front, began the final plan for the Battle of the Somme. They had a formidable army at their disposal. In August 1914, a British force of four infantry divisions and one cavalry division had been sent to defend Belgium. Now, nearly two years later, Haig had overall command of four armies, made up of 58 divisions. Most of these men were "Kitchener's Army" recruits who had joined in 1914. Now they were trained and ready to fight, they were keen to show what they could do.

Right from the start, there was something

painfully unimaginative about the tactics Haig and Rawlinson proposed, although Haig was convinced God had helped him with his battle plans. The date for opening the attack was July 1, at 7:30 in the morning, after a five-day bombardment by 1,350 artillery guns. It was all too obvious to the enemy. The five-day bombardment indicated a forthcoming attack in that sector as clearly as a skywriting biplane.

Those who had rushed to join up, in the first flush of enthusiasm for the war, were about to find out the true nature of 20th-century warfare. On the evening before the attack, the soldiers destined to take part in the first day of the battle were taken to front-line trenches. With extraordinary thoughtlessness, some squads of men were marched past open mass graves, freshly dug in anticipation of the heavy casualties to come. Then, as close to the enemy as most of them had ever been, they tried to settle into their uncomfortable final positions, and to ready themselves for the next morning. Sleep, with the artillery bombardment reaching a cacophonous peak, was quite impossible.

On the day before the beginning of the offensive, the commanding officers had briefed their men on the task ahead. They had been told that the trenches they were to attack would be virtually undefended – the five-day bombardment would have seen to that, and would also have cut the barbed wire in front of the German trenches to pieces. So confident were the generals that their men would have no problems taking the German front line that troops were sent into battle with 30kg (66lbs) or more of equipment – equivalent in weight to two heavy suitcases. This was because they were expected to occupy the German front lines and repel any counterattacks.

The Somme was not a good place to launch an attack. The major reason for its chosen location – the joining point of the British and French front lines – had been reduced to a minor consideration after Verdun. Now, only five French divisions were going to take part in the battle, along with 14 British ones. But, all along the front, the Germans occupied higher ground, forcing the British to advance uphill. The chalk ground had also made it easier for the Germans to dig 12m (40ft) underground, constructing heavily fortified positions that were mostly immune to the massive bombardment.

The five days of shelling was not as impressive as it sounded, either. The one and a half million shells fired had been produced in haste, and quality control had slipped considerably. Many were duds which never exploded. And, rather than making the attack easier, the bombardment churned up the ground in front of the German trenches, making it much more difficult to pass through.

The British artillery bombardment ended at 7:30 that morning. Then, several huge explosions rocked the German trenches. Explosives had been placed in mines dug at intervals under German positions along the 28km (18 miles) of the front designated for the attack. Following this mountainous explosion of earth, a strange silence settled over the battlefield. After the constant roar of the last five days, it seemed quite unnatural. The German soldiers knew immediately that something was about to happen. They quickly emerged from their deep bunkers and set up their machine guns.

All along the battlefront, whistles blew: the signal to attack. Troops climbed up wooden ladders placed along the outer edge of the front-line trenches. They arranged themselves into the neat lines they had learned to form in training, and waded into No Man's Land in successive waves. Some battalions had tin discs pinned to their backs, to glint in the sun. The idea was to show the artillery where they were, so they wouldn't get hit by shells falling short. It was a bright summer morning, already so hot the men could feel the heat of the sun on the backs of their necks.

It was Rawlinson's plan of action that called for the soldiers to advance in straight lines to a precise timetable. Other tactics had been discussed. Haig had suggested sending advance parties to check that the wire had been destroyed. But Rawlinson rejected such ideas. He thought his inexperienced troops were incapable of following anything but the simplest plan. There was to be no flexibility or initiative, just momentum. He intended a vast, sprawling tide of men to sweep the Germans from their positions.

The first wave advanced. As they approached the German lines, those leading the attack saw to their horror that the barbed wire had not been destroyed at all. The British artillery shells had just blown the barbed wire into the air, and it had settled back again where it had previously been. There were gaps in the wire, but these had been deliberately left by the Germans to herd attacking enemy troops into "killing zones", where German machine-gun fire was concentrated at its heaviest.

According to Allied thinking, any Germans who survived the bombardment were supposed to have become disoriented and overwhelmed by the sheer size of the force sent against them. But, instead, they just got on with the grisly business of butchering their attackers. They set up their machine guns — alarmingly effective weapons that could fire 600 bullets a minute — and mowed down the approaching British troops like swathes of corn before the scythe.

In one famous incident, a captain in the Eighth Battalion, East Surrey Regiment, gave the signal to attack by climbing onto the rim of his trench and kicking a football in the direction of the enemy lines. No doubt he was trying to allay the fears of his men with a show of devil-may-care bravado. But he was killed almost instantly, somewhat undermining the effect he was trying to create.

One of the soldiers sent in to attack that day was Henry Williamson, who survived the battle and went on to become a writer – *Tarka the Otter* being among his most famous works. He also wrote about his experiences in the war, and described the horror of taking part in the attack with haunting vividness: "I see men arising and walking forward and I go forward with them, in a glassy delirium," he recorded. All around him, his fellow soldiers fell to the ground – some almost gently, others rolling and screaming with fear. Williamson pressed on through ground he described as resembling "a huge ruined honeycomb". He watched, miraculously unscathed, as his comrades were shot to pieces. Three other waves came up behind him to meet the same pitiful fate. Londoner Arthur Wagstaff, who also went over the top at 7:30 that Saturday morning, recalled the opening minutes more simply: "We looked along the line and we realized there were very few of us left."

In accordance with the plan, the attack went on all morning, with four waves of men going out to the same grim fate. The British army was probably the most rigid and inflexible fighting force of the war. Junior officers in the heat of battle were expected to obey their orders to the letter, even if they found themselves in almost impossible circumstances. Communications between the officers at the Front and the generals at the rear of the battle were poor too, dependent as they were on telephone lines, which would often be broken by shellfire, and runners, who carried messages from the Front to the rear, and were often killed. Soldiers and their officers had been briefed to go forward at any cost, and this they did, despite the obvious futility of doing so. Field Marshal Haig and General Rawlinson might as well have been marching their men straight over a cliff.

By early afternoon, news of the slaughter trickled back to army headquarters, and further attacks that day were called off. The casualty figures were the worst for any single day in the history of the British army, and the worst for any day, in any army, of the entire war.

Back at the casualty clearing stations to the rear of the front, men who had returned from No Man's Land milled around in confusion, searching for a familiar face. Then came the ritual of the roll call, which established who had returned from the attack and who had not.

"So many of our friends were missing, and obviously had been killed or wounded," remembered Tommy Gay, of the Royal Scots Fusiliers, interviewed for a TV documentary shortly before he died in 1999. "All those bullets," he recalled. "All those bullets, and not one with my name on... I was the luckiest man in the world."

Of the 120,000 men who took part in the first morning's fighting, half were casualties. There were 20,000 killed, and another 40,000 wounded. That night, a slow trickle of men who had been injured in No Man's Land, and who had spent the day hiding in shell craters under the hot sun, managed to return to their trenches under cover of darkness.

The way the attack was reported in the British press sheds an interesting light on the way news was managed during the war. One newspaper painted a picture of the opening day of the battle as a great victory, and described the disaster as "a good day for England." Another wrote of "a slow, continuous and methodical push, sparing in lives". No doubt such reports offered reassurance to anxious families at home, but they made the soldiers who had taken part in such attacks deeply angry.

Some battalions had come through with few casualties, but others had suffered terribly. The Second Battalion, Middlesex Regiment, for example, had started the day with 24 officers, and 650 men. At roll call that evening, only a single officer and 50 men remained. The Accrington Pals, who were among the first to attack the German line that morning, lost 584 men out of 720 – killed, wounded or simply vanished – in the first half hour of the battle. Despite the total lack of reliable news from the front, their families at home in Lancashire began to suspect something terrible had happened to their men. The regular flow of letters from France suddenly stopped. A week after the battle started, a train full of wounded soldiers from the Somme briefly stopped at Accrington station on the way to an army hospital further north. One man on the train called out to a group of women on the platform, "Where are we?" When they told him, he said, "Accrington...The Accrington Pals! They've been wiped out!" News spread quickly, and an awful atmosphere, like dull, heavy air before a thunderstorm, hung over the town. Then, letters from wounded men assuring their families that they were still alive began to arrive. The letters came in such numbers, it was obvious that something really big had happened. Those who received no such letter were left in a dreadful limbo – should they hope for the best or fear the worst?

Aware that its readers were desperate for information, the local paper *The Accrington Observer* knew the story could wait no longer. But it concealed the real news in heroic hyperbole, typical of the style of the day. "What is certain is the Pals Battalion has won for itself a glorious page in the record of dauntless courage and imperishable valour," said the *Observer*, before it went on to admit, "the dead and wounded are more numerous than we would fain [willingly] have hoped."

Then, agonizingly slowly, over the next six weeks, official War Office letters began to arrive at homes throughout the town, confirming the deaths of those killed on the first day of the Somme. For the whole summer, the *Observer* was filled with row upon row of photos of those who had died. The town was devastated, as the fatal flaw in the idea of the Pals battalions made itself apparent. When men in battle were slaughtered on such a scale, entire towns would be thrown into mourning.

There was to be something even worse about the Somme than 60,000 casualties in a single morning. Despite the losses, Haig and Rawlinson remained convinced their failure lay in not sending in enough men – they thought the big push had not been big enough. So, for the next five months, the volunteers of "Kitchener's Army" were poured into a hideous grinding machine to be destroyed in their thousands, caught in barbed wire and lashed by machine-gun bullets.

There were a few successes amid the carnage. A night attack on July 14 caught the Germans by surprise, and 8km (5 miles) of front-line German trenches were overrun. Next morning, this breakthrough was followed up by a cavalry charge – the standard tactic used in 19th-century warfare when the enemy's front line had been pierced. The cavalry men did not look quite as dashing as they once did; their red jackets had been replaced by dreary khaki. Bugles still blew and lances glittered in the hot, summer sun. Like all cavalry charges, it was a magnificent sight. But it ended in a hail of machine-gun bullets, flailing hooves and twitching bodies.

Australian troops made their debut on the Western Front, and fought with great courage. Three weeks into the battle, they captured the village of Pozières. But they paid a terrible price for their victory. So many were killed, one soldier described it as "the heaviest, bloodiest, rottenest stunt that ever

Australians were caught up in."

On September 15, 1916, tanks were employed for the first time in history. The British pinned great hopes on these new weapons; "machine gun destroyers" they called them. Indeed, for a German machine gunner in his trench, there was nothing quite so terrifying as facing a huge tank, metal tracks clanking and grinding as it lumbered forward to crush his defensive barbed wire, with bullets bouncing off its heavy steel flank. The tank would eventually prove to be one of the most effective weapons of the century – but not at the Battle of the Somme. Most broke down before they could even reach the front line.

After 140 days, when the battle finally ground to a halt in November 1916, over a million men had been killed or wounded. In all, there were 420,000 British casualties, 200,000 French and 450,000 German. The defenders, mainly men of the German Second Army, suffered so many casualties because their own general, Fritz von Below, had decreed that any ground gained by the British or French had to be recaptured at all cost. "I forbid the voluntary evacuation of trenches," he said. "The will to stand firm must be impressed on every man in the Army... The enemy should have to carve his way over heaps of corpses."

Having been mown down in their thousands attacking front-line German trenches, the Allied soldiers exacted a grim revenge, as the enemy exposed themselves to similar carnage in an effort to win back lost ground. "You've given it to us, now we're going to give it to you... Our machine gunners had a whale of a time," recalled one British soldier.

Any positive military advantage from this whirlwind of destruction was almost unnoticeable. In some areas along the 28km (18-mile) Front, the front line had been redrawn by 8km (5 miles) here or there. But, like so many other battles of the First World War, death on such an industrial scale had not served any useful purpose. Soldiers in the British army would never show such misplaced enthusiasm for battle again. From then on, ordinary soldiers would refer to the campaign on the Somme with a bitter and heartfelt loathing.

To this day, the horror, naiveté and carnage of the early hours of that Saturday morning still shocks anyone who studies the war. For those who

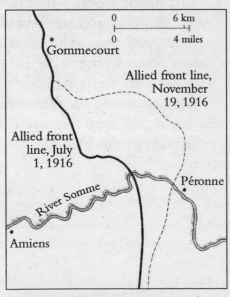

The front line on the Somme

took part and survived, it would be the defining moment of their lives. One survivor, Sergeant J.E. Yates of the West Yorkshire Regiment, recalled the effects the first day of battle had on him:

"Almost imperceptibly, the first day merged into the second, when we held grimly to a battered trench and watched each other grow old under the day-long storm of shelling. For hours, sweating, praying, swearing we worked on the heaps of chalk and mangled bodies. Men did astonishing things at which one did not wonder till after... At dawn next morning we were back in a green wood. I found myself leaning on a rifle and staring stupidly at the filthy exhausted men who slept round me. It did not occur to me to lie down until someone pushed me into a bed of ferns. There were flowers among the ferns, and my last thought was a dull wonder that there could still be flowers in the world."

The quiet rebellion

May-June 1917

During the First World War, trench soldiers on both sides faced a kind of warfare that no one before or since has had to fight. Every day promised soldiers a gruesome death or injury from sniper fire and artillery bombardment. Once or twice a year, there would be a "big push" that tended to kill at least half the men they knew. And, along with the danger, there was the barren panorama of No Man's Land and the unending hardship of the trenches.

Ice and snow, rain and mud, baking heat — whatever the weather, a trench was no place for men to be. Rats gnawed at their dead companions, they were perpetually plagued with lice, and any sort of plumbing system for the daily effluent of hundreds of thousands of front-line troops was clearly out of the question. In this tortured landscape, with the hideous stench of excrement and rotting corpses, the war went on, and on, and on... until those fighting believed it would go on forever. "O Jesus, make it stop!" was the heartfelt plea ending British front-line officer Siegfried Sassoon's 1918 poem "Attack".

But not all soldiers were prepared to carry on

fighting. The British and American armies avoided any major outbreaks of rebellion, but every other major fighting nation had its share. Naval mutinies in Germany occurred in 1917 and at the end of the war. Some Austro-Hungarian troops fighting on the Eastern Front mutinied as early as 1915. Most critical of all, Russian soldiers deserted and mutinied in droves, and brought on the revolutions of 1917 which led to Russia's withdrawal from the war.

The French army mutinied too, in the spring and early summer of 1917. It was a decisive moment that could have cost France the war. Fortunately, the German generals didn't believe the reports they received from spies and prisoners of war about the mutiny. By the time they realized it was really happening, the mutiny was over.

The word "mutiny" conjures up images of drunken violence and a descent into anarchy. It is a

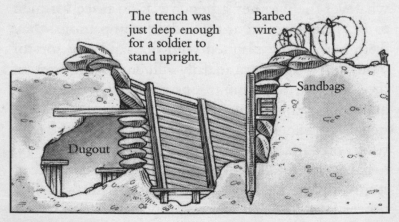

The trench was just deep enough for a soldier to stand upright.

Barbed wire

Sandbags

Dugout

Inside a trench

word to make an officer's blood run cold. For, without order and obedience, one man cannot tell other men to carry out actions that will undoubtedly result in death and injury. Mutiny renders an army ineffective more surely than a curtain of machine-gun fire or an artillery barrage. It can lead to utter defeat in a matter of days, so it is usually punished with great severity. In ancient Rome, mutinous army legions that had returned to military discipline were subject to "decimation" – one man in ten was plucked from the ranks and executed. Who could ever have guessed that this ancient, barbaric remedy would be employed again in the 20th century, to restore order to one of Europe's greatest armies?

The French mutinies of 1917 had their roots in German general Erich von Falkenhayn's decision to fight the war by taking French lives rather than French territory. In February 1916, he chose the French fortress of Verdun to do this. In a horrendous 10-month battle, the French and Germans fought for possession of this stronghold. Much of the fighting took place in dank, concrete forts awash with blood, and steeped in the stark terror of men in hand-to-hand combat. When the battle ended in December that year, 350,000 French soldiers and 330,000 German soldiers had been killed or injured. There was nothing to show for all this slaughter. No territory had been won or lost. Each side had lost an almost equal number of troops. Falkenhayn was dismissed from his post. But his declared aim of "bleeding the French army white" had had more of an effect than he realized.

The French people were immensely proud of their army's success in defending Verdun, and the soldier's terse battle cry, *"Ils ne passeront pas."* ("They shall not pass.") became a slogan of national self-esteem. The two generals held most responsible for fending off the Germans, Philippe Pétain and Robert Nivelle, became national heroes. But, after Verdun, many French soldiers who had fought there felt they had nothing left to give.

Another major French offensive was planned in the early spring of 1917. Nivelle, still basking in his success, promised the troops a quick victory at Chemin des Dames, on the River Aisne. This, he told his men, would be the battle that would win the war. Morale was high, especially as the French soldiers were told they would be trying out a new tactic sure to save lives. They would head over to the German trenches under the protection of a "creeping barrage" – a hail of shells which would fall in front of them, gradually advancing like a protective wall of fire. Tanks would be used too – a new type of weapon which promised to crush defensive barbed wire and destroy the deadly machine-gun nests, which could sweep away scores of men with a single burst of fire.

A million men took part in the attack on April 16. It failed pitifully, and the same senseless slaughter ensued. The tanks broke down and the artillery bombardment failed to destroy the enemy strongpoints. The weather didn't help; the French soldiers often had to advance in driving rain. After 10 days, 34,000 men had been killed, with 20,000 missing, almost certainly dead too. Another 90,000 had been wounded. But still the attacks continued.

Not all the soldiers had believed Nivelle's promises of an easy victory and decisive breakthrough. In fact, some companies of men had marched to the front line bleating like sheep, believing they were lambs to the slaughter. It was a warning sign that was carelessly ignored. Chemin des Dames became the place where the morale of the French army finally broke.

Nivelle's career was over. Already seriously ill with tuberculosis, he would not live to see the end of the war. His replacement was the other hero of Verdun, Pétain. He moved from his post of chief of the French general staff, to become commander-in-chief of the French northern and northeast armies. Pétain had only been in his new job for three days when he received reports of mutinies among front-line soldiers.

The first occurred in the 2nd Battalion of the 18th Infantry Regiment. Out of 600 men, only 200 had survived the Chemin des Dames offensive. After a brief respite behind the French front lines, they were once again ordered back to the trenches. It was the early evening of April 29, 1917. Many of the men were drunk on the cheap red wine that was supplied free, and frequently, to French troops. Almost all refused to return, gathering in large groups and shouting "Down with the war!" But, by early the next morning, the men had sobered up, and marched back to the front line.

As they marched, the officers of the battalion decided this insurrection should be immediately punished. At random, a dozen men were pulled from the ranks and charged with mutiny. Five of them were shot. Another had an amazing escape. As he was being led to the firing squad by a group of guards, a German artillery bombardment fell around them. He ran into nearby woods and was never seen again.

Four days later, another mutiny broke out. This was far more serious as it involved the entire Second Division – thousands of men, almost all drunk and refusing to carry their weapons or go back to the trenches. But, when the drink wore off, most of the men gave in and marched to the Front. The few who still refused to go were quickly arrested, and no one else in the division was singled out for punishment.

It was just the beginning. In early May, this drunken rebellion spread throughout the army. It was an odd sort of mutiny, though. There were no reports of officers being attacked or killed, and no political demands. When officers spoke to the men who had been elected by their comrades to represent them, they were told the soldiers would continue to defend their trenches. It was the attacks against the Germans they were no longer prepared to take part in.

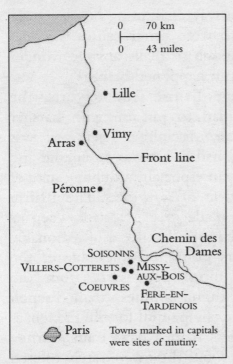

0   70 km
0   43 miles

• Lille

• Vimy
Arras •

Front line

Péronne •

Chemin des
Dames
SOISONNS
VILLERS-COTTERETS • • MISSY-
AUX-BOIS
COEUVRES
FERE-EN-
TARDENOIS

Paris   Towns marked in capitals
were sites of mutiny.

Map of the 1917 French mutinies

While large-scale mutiny swept the ranks of the French army, extraordinary events were taking place in Russia, where a similarly widespread mutiny had led to the overthrow of the Tsarist government, deeply alarming the other Allies. The French authorities were lucky there were no equivalents of Lenin or Trotsky among their troops; if there had been, the history of France, and Europe, over the course of the 20th century might have been very different. The French rebellion had no obvious leaders and was not being directed by anyone. But, despite this, the mutiny spread so fast that by June, 54 divisions – over half the entire French army on the Western Front – were affected. Some 30,000 men just left their front-line posts and tried to walk home.

The causes of the mutiny were both simple and complicated. In essence, the ordinary French soldier had lost faith in his generals. He was not prepared to lay down his life for a way of fighting he no longer believed in. But there were other causes too, and these were serious enough to make anyone wonder why the mutiny had not happened before.

Compared to their British counterparts, the French soldiers had had to put up with harsher conditions and military discipline. Their pay was miserly. The food they had to eat was often cold and of very poor quality – an especially troubling state of affairs for such a nation of gourmets. The British army, by comparison, made great efforts to keep its trench soldiers supplied with hot food of reasonable quality. British soldiers from the other side of the Channel also spent more time away from the trenches, and with their families, than French soldiers. This was especially painful for the French, as many were fighting less than a day's train journey away from their homes; but they were rarely offered leave. Although all sides suffered horrendous casualties, of the Allies, the French lost the most men. One in four Frenchmen between the ages of 18 and 30 would die in the war – a million and a half in all, with millions more wounded and maimed for life.

In the French High Command, the mutiny caused a sense of panic. France had already suffered so much – so many men had been sacrificed to keep the German army from overrunning their country. How awful it would be if the French lost the war because their troops had just given up and gone home.

Pétain, as commander-in-chief of the mutinous divisions, was the man who had to sort it all out. Fortunately for France, he chose to address his soldiers' complaints, rather than simply to suppress the revolt with great brutality. He had three major problems. First, he had to take immediate steps to introduce reforms to make life more bearable for his men, most of whom were conscripts fighting for the duration of the war, rather than career soldiers. Second, in order to uphold discipline in the army, he had to punish those responsible – a difficult task when the mutiny really did seem to be spontaneous and lacking in "ring leaders". Third, and most important of all, he had to keep the mutiny secret from the Germans. If they knew what was going on, they could break through the French lines and be in Paris within a week. Then the war would be lost for sure.

Several older generals were immediately replaced. The quality of food fed to front-line troops was improved. A system of home leave was introduced, and rest camps behind the front lines were made more habitable. The arrival of Pétain, although it happened just before the mutinies occurred, was a stroke of luck. This veteran French general, already 60 years old in 1917, had a reputation for being careful with the lives of his men. Almost alone among the officers of the French High Command, ordinary soldiers trusted him not to throw away their lives in useless offensives.

Nonetheless, punishment for the mutiny was random and transparently unfair. For example, in early June, a battalion of 700 men under the command of General Emile Taufflieb was marching back to the Front when they all disappeared into a forest at the side of the road. Earlier in the day, word had swept through the troops that there was a vast cave nearby in which they could all hide. Taufflieb, showing commendable bravery, went into the cave and talked to the mutineers. He told them to return to the front by daybreak, or they would all be slaughtered. The men came out. But once they were back under army command, 20 were pulled from the ranks and shot. Taufflieb had neglected to mention this would happen. But, in other divisions, once order had been restored, the momentary mutiny was swiftly forgotten and no one was punished.

In all, perhaps 24,000 men were arrested and put before military courts. Of these, 554 judged to be leaders of the revolt were sentenced to death. But only 45 were shot; the rest were sent to the penal colony of French Guiana – a miserable fate for conscripted soldiers who had fought bravely until they could take no more. Those executed were shot before their comrades, who were then made to file past the dead men. Many more French soldiers were shot at random and without trial, but the number of those deaths is difficult to estimate.

The mutiny was dealt with carefully. But, beneath the concern, there was an iron fist determined that such widespread disobedience would never be allowed to happen again. Among the rebellious divisions was a regiment of Russian soldiers, sent to the Western Front as a goodwill gesture by the ailing Tsarist regime before it was overthrown. These soldiers had endured even worse conditions and even more incompetent leadership than their French and British allies. They were all too ready to follow their rebellious French comrades and mutiny. Their fate was pitiful. The French authorities had had to deal with their own soldiers with some leniency – there were too many to punish, and harsh discipline might have provoked worse rebellions, and even revolution. The Russians, though, were expendable. The regiment was surrounded and blown to pieces by French artillery.

The mutiny had lasted for six weeks. The French army had escaped a crushing defeat by the skin of its teeth. But the soldiers who had rebelled had sent a clear message to their generals. From now on, there would be no more mass attacks; French soldiers would only take part in small-scale assaults on the German lines. And so the horrific bloodletting of the previous three years came to an end. For the rest of the war, the lion's share of the fighting against the Central Powers would be left to Britain and the Commonwealth, and fresh and enthusiastic American troops, who had entered the war just in time to save the Allies from an almost certain defeat.

Behind the front lines, the government reacted by tightening censorship in the French newspapers and imprisoning those who had campaigned for an end to the war. These days, such people would be called peace campaigners. In 1917, they were called anti-war agitators.

Even now, the mutiny is still a shameful and touchy subject in France. On its 80th anniversary in 1997, the French prime minister, Lionel Jospin, suggested the mutineers needed to be understood and forgiven. This provoked a stern denunciation from the French president, Jacques Chirac. The act of expressing sympathy for those war-weary men was still considered an outrage. But, nowadays, most people would agree that the mutineers deserved pity rather than condemnation. They were, said French politician François Hollande recently, "simply men who got lost in a hell of fire and blood."

The cellar house of Pervyse

1914-1918

Elizabeth "Elsie" Knocker and Mairi Chisholm were not used to such deprivation. Elsie, a young widow of 24, and Mairi, only 18, were sleeping on straw surrounded by a bunch of filthy, ragged soldiers. Three months earlier, theirs had been a world of grand houses, servants, fine china plates and strictly observed etiquette. But the world had turned. Now they were volunteer nurses attached to the Belgian army, in headlong retreat before the German army, and taking shelter in a derelict cellar in the Belgian village of Oudecappelle.

Elsie found sleep impossible. Rats scurried around her head, and the men snored horribly. She got up slowly, and gingerly picked her way through the outstretched limbs of the sleeping soldiers, out into the cold, bright moonlight. Hours before, this landscape had been subjected to an artillery barrage, which had left many houses in ruins. But now all was silent. The air was still dusty from the bombardment, but felt like a crystal mountain breeze after the fetid atmosphere of the cellar. As she stood breathing in great lungfuls, she heard a sound behind her. There, stumbling through the rubble, was Mairi, come to join her.

Close by, an artillery bombardment started up, sending shells over to the German lines and shaking the ground beneath their feet. A biting wind blew in from the sea, and the two women hugged each other tight for warmth. To the east, a thin band of light on the horizon cast a sickly glow on the ruined village.

In the first light of dawn, they decided they were in this horrible jam for the long term, and they had better get used to it. Taking a pair of surgical scissors, Mairi cut away Elsie's dark, silky hair, leaving her with a short, two-inch crop. Elsie did the same for Mairi's long, fair hair. Then they gathered up the shorn locks and threw them into the canal that ran close to their shelter. In Edwardian times, at the start of the 20th century, a woman's long hair was an absolutely central part of her beauty – her "crowning glory". So it was a gesture of infinite significance to cut it off. Elsie later recalled: "With that bundle of hair went all our nervousness, all our fear of rats, our dislike of dirty food, and our ideas of home comforts. We became soldiers from that hour."

Soon after, they posed together for a photograph. Standing stiffly in their khaki overalls, high riding boots and nurse's hats, their determination is clear. Elsie, tall and fragile, stares sternly at the camera. She looks sad, large dark eyes peering from her gaunt face, wisps of black hair curling around the edge of her hat. Mairi called her "Gypsy" because of her dark looks. Elsie was a sensitive woman, but that didn't stop her from expressing strong opinions, and she did not suffer fools gladly. The photo shows Mairi as shorter and stockier, a hint of a smile playing around her mouth. She looks very young, but formidably determined. She was, noted a friend, the kind of woman who "cannot bear to sit down in an untidy room". They made a good team. But how did these two young women come to find themselves in such circumstances?

At the beginning of the 20th century, there were strict conventions about what was right and proper for a woman to do. Most men had deep prejudices about women's capabilities. Many women accepted that they should live within these narrow boundaries. But these were changing times, and the war would make a considerable difference to women's lives.

In the years before the war, a mass political movement of feminists, including the Suffragettes, had campaigned for the right for women to vote – as the vote was then only available to men. When war broke out, the movement suspended its activities and threw its support behind the government and the country. Voluntary women's organizations were formed, especially to help sick and wounded soldiers both behind the front line in France and as they slowly recovered. Huge numbers of women came forward to volunteer to work as nurses and ambulance drivers, and to set up soup kitchens and field canteens to feed troops. There was a strict ban on allowing women in the front line, though.

Things were changing at home, too. Men in the Territorial Army (part-time soldiers), and those who had rushed to join up at the start of the war, left their jobs to go to fight. When casualties mounted and the army could no longer rely on volunteers to replace their missing numbers, conscription was introduced. This created hitherto undreamed of employment opportunities for women, who flocked into previously male-only occupations to fill the gaps in the workforce. At first, the sight of women bus drivers or conductors was considered faintly shocking. But, by the time the war was over, thousands of women throughout Europe were working. Many of these jobs were in factories such as munitions works, producing shells and bullets. Women even worked in the coal mines. But the old attitudes still died hard. Throughout the war, women continued to face absurd prejudices. Even in 1917, the British newspaper *The Daily Telegraph* was running headlines asking such questions as: "Are women capable of driving at night?"

What Elsie Knocker and Mairi Chisholm did in Belgium would be remarkable even today. When the war broke out, Elsie, a trained nurse, went at once to London to offer her services to the authorities. Arriving in the capital, she was caught up in a wave of frantic planning and excitement. Committees were set up to get women volunteers to the war zone as quickly as possible, as nurses and ambulance drivers. But all these plans were curtly rejected by both the War Office (the government department responsible for the army) and the British Red Cross. To be fair, some of the schemes were hare-brained, such as the one that envisaged nurses on horseback being sent out to scour the battlefields for wounded soldiers. Ideas like this belonged firmly to the previous century. They had no place in the shell craters and barbed wire of the No Man's Land between the trenches. But few people in the summer of 1914 had any idea what the war would actually be like. Most were convinced it would be a great adventure.

Elsie was determined not to "wait for a bunch of men to tell me what to do". She had heard of a volunteer organization called the Flying Ambulance Corps, which was going straight out to Belgium. When she presented her credentials, they snapped her up. She was not only a trained nurse, but an expert driver and a mechanic too – unusual skills for a woman in 1914. At this time, only the rich could afford cars, so many women from wealthy backgrounds put their motoring skills to use driving ambulances.

The corps had been founded by a Scottish doctor, Hector Munro, whom Elsie described affectionately, but sharply, as "an eccentric Scottish specialist, one whose primary object seemed to be leadership of the feminist crusade, for he was far keener on women's

rights than most of the women he recruited."
According to Elsie, "he was a likeable man and a
brilliant impresario, but wonderfully vague in matters
of detail, and in appearance the very essence of an
absent-minded professor".

Perhaps it was because of Munro's transparent
eccentricity, but the services of his Flying Ambulance
Corps were rejected, not only by the War Office and
the British Red Cross, but the French and American
Red Cross too. But the Belgian Red Cross wasn't so
fussy – perhaps because their country was in the thick
of the German invasion.

Along with Munro, two other doctors, a couple of
drivers and an army chaplain, Elsie and a handful of
women volunteer nurses set off across the Channel
for Belgium. Among the nurses was Mairi Chisholm,
whom Elsie had known before the war. They had
met again in London while doing volunteer dispatch
riding for the Women's Emergency Corps, another
new organization set up at the start of the war. Mairi
was an enthusiastic and fearless motorcyclist. She
rode down to London as soon as war broke out, to
offer her help. She had no knowledge of nursing, but
was confident she could pick up what she needed to
know "on the job".

Because they were not part of any government-
approved organization, the members of Munro's
ambulance corps had to finance their own
expedition. The women bought their own clothes,
including heavy khaki overcoats, high lace-up boots

and riding breeches. Elsie had inherited some money when her husband died, which paid her expenses. Mairi came from a wealthy background, but went to Belgium in the teeth of fierce parental disapproval. She had to sell her motorbike to pay for her clothing and travel costs. They might have been forgiven if they had felt indignant about having to pay their own way – after all, they were offering to risk their lives to aid the Allies in the war. But they were determined to put the best possible spin on everything. As Elsie said: "We preferred to be financially independent. It gave us greater freedom of movement, and spared us some of the annoyances of red tape."

The Flying Ambulance Corps set up in Ghent, a little behind the Belgian front line, and made themselves immensely useful. They cared for wounded soldiers, and carried cocoa and soup out to the front-line soldiers. Their work was often hair-raisingly dangerous. On one occasion, Elsie and Mairi rescued a wounded Belgian officer in a village that was being overrun by German soldiers. As they attended to him and other wounded men, hand-to-hand fighting was taking place a mere block away.

But Elsie quickly spotted a major problem with their work. Many wounded soldiers died while being transported to medical posts safely behind the front lines. Wouldn't it be better, she thought, if they could receive medical attention right next to the actual fighting? Mairi agreed. So, after two months behind the front, they set out to find a suitable spot nearer the trenches. By this time, almost all of Belgium had been overrun by the German army, and only a small triangle of territory near the Channel coast remained in Belgian hands. Right behind the front line was a small village called Pervyse – and here they made their base.

The route to Pervyse was littered with enough portents to convince even the least superstitious visitor to turn around and go back. It was lucky that Elsie and Marie were too sensible to believe in omens. As they drove through mud and past shell holes, the side of the road was marked by the bloated bodies of dead cows, sheep and horses, all killed in murderous artillery bombardments or caught in the crossfire of combat. Some of these carcasses had been left to rot, others stripped of meat by soldiers desperate for a meal. Then, at less regular intervals, but frequent enough to remind them of the terrible danger they were placing themselves in, there were burned-out vehicles. Some still had the charred, mangled remains of their passengers inside them.

Pervyse was as grim as the route that led to it. Many of its stone houses had been destroyed by shells, and all the trees around the village had withered. The church was peppered with holes and the graveyard had been churned up, with long-dead bodies poking through the broken ground. As if this was not enough to despoil the scene, the low-lying land had been flooded during the German advance. Dank seawater had mixed with the freshwater of the canals and rivers, and dead freshwater fish killed by the salt lay rotting on the surface.

It was here, in late November of 1914, that they found a derelict house, and set up a medical post in its cellar. The room was a mere 3m x 2.5m (12ft by 10ft) and without any facilities. The house had been quite handsome in its time, but now the roof was in tatters and every window pane was smashed. A stove was found in a nearby house and dragged over to the cellar. Straw was spread on the floor to sleep on. Water was brought in from wherever it could be found. Not only did they need it to drink and cook with, but it was also essential to use for boiling water to sterilize surgical implements. There was barely more than "a teaspoon" left for them to wash.

With them in this first outpost were two men supplied by the Belgian army. One was a driver (although both women could drive); the other was a cook. All four slept in the straw of their cellar, surviving as best they could on food they would never have dreamed of eating a few months before. Most of it was soup. It was either terribly thin – "one tomato and 15 pints of water", as Mairi tartly observed – or thick and swimming in fat, which floated unappetizingly on the surface.

Positioned directly behind the front line, they were in constant danger from artillery fire and stray bullets. There was also the ever-present possibility that the

German army would break through the Belgian trenches and overrun the town. But such was the static nature of the fighting that the two women were able to remain in this village, just behind the front line, for almost the entire war.

When they first arrived, the village had only been partially destroyed by the fighting. But, as the war progressed, the whole place fell into dereliction. A big convent was totally destroyed, and the church was razed to the ground. One part of the village by a road junction became known as "Suicide Corner", because shell fire was particularly intense there.

Sometimes, during lulls in artillery barrages, the women would venture into No Man's Land, to search for wounded soldiers in the churned-up mud. If they found anyone, they would carry the man on their shoulders back to the medical post. Such work was extraordinarily dangerous, because they were plainly visible to the German trenches and could easily have been shot at by German soldiers.

After a few months, the cellar became unbearably cramped, so the two moved their medical post to another house in the village. But this too was semi-derelict, with half the roof missing. While they were away from the house, German artillery destroyed it, so another spot was found nearby. This medical post proved the best yet, and they were able to stay there for the rest of their time at the front. Over the months, and with help from Belgian soldiers, the two women took considerable steps to protect themselves and their patients. A fortified concrete blockhouse was built in the house, and they worked inside it. The outside of the house was covered in sandbags to protect them from the blast of shells exploding nearby.

Running the medical post cost money, of course, and Mairi and Elsie had to fund their activities by occasional visits back to Britain to collect money for their work. Although the Belgian authorities did not offer to finance them, the army supplied soldiers to help with the driving and the care of wounded men. But, more often than not, such helpers were unfit for front-line combat, so were of limited use.

As Elsie and Mairi were the only two women on the Western Front to work so close to the trenches, they became quite well-known. Newspapers referred to them as "the Heroines of Pervyse" and, in February 1915, King Albert of the Belgians visited Pervyse to present them personally with the Belgian Order of Leopold – a medal given in recognition of their bravery.

Most days were a dizzy succession of catastrophes and tragedies. Although many casualties were men injured by shells or bullets, others were soldiers who were suffering from illnesses caused by living in the open trenches: frostbite, "trenchfoot" (a form of frostbite) and bronchitis. When there was a lull in the fighting, and the stream of casualties coming to their door slowed, Elsie and Mairi would forage for cabbages and potatoes in the nearby fields, to make soup for the soldiers. Occasionally they would return with shrapnel holes in their clothing but, amazingly, both escaped injury. On one occasion, Elsie was watching a Belgian doctor approaching the medical post. Suddenly, a shell fell from the sky and he vanished in a flash of dirty brown earth. How they kept going for so long is a mystery. They were up at six o'clock every morning, to make hot chocolate or coffee for the men in the nearby trenches and, when they were not cooking, they were nursing.

Once their patients had been given first aid, it was Mairi's and Elsie's responsibility to drive them to a hospital well behind the front lines. This was extremely difficult and dangerous. The roads on the 24km (15 mile) journey were often deep in mud and littered with shell craters. The ambulance often came under heavy fire too, even at night when most of the driving was undertaken. Frequently, the vehicle would slide off the road to become stuck in a ditch or hole, and Mairi would have to ask passing soldiers to help her push it out.

Driving at night in such conditions, with no lights, took special skill and was extremely stressful. Whenever the ambulance skidded off the road, the badly injured men would tumble around in the back of the vehicle, often screaming in agony. Sometimes, Mairi would make two or three such journeys a night, and return to her bed with "eyes on stalks, bloodshot and strained... I never felt so googly [exhausted] and utterly played out in my life," she later wrote.

As the war progressed, the village lay in ruins, although Mairi felt it had a strange kind of beauty in the moonlight. All around them were the horrors of war. Corpses floated in vast pools of stagnant water, and occasionally the arms or legs of men torn to pieces by shell fire were found just lying in the road. By the end of the war, little remained of the village except rubble and gable ends.

But, in these dreadful circumstances, Elsie Knocker fell in love. She met a Belgian pilot named Baron Harold de T'Serclaes. In early 1916, they married and Mrs. Knocker became the Baroness de T'Serclaes. At first, Mairi thought the relationship would take her friend away, but Elsie continued to work closely with her at their medical post.

In 1917, the two were summoned to rescue a British pilot who had crashed in No Man's Land. He was badly injured and in need of urgent medical attention. Risking their lives, they managed to arrange a truce with German soldiers, and brought the pilot safely back. For this they were awarded the British Military Medal — another decoration recognizing their immense courage.

In an effort to raise funds for their project, the two women gave their letters and diaries to a friend, who wrote an account of their adventures called *The*

Cellar House of Pervyse. On the final page, a pink insert pleads with the purchaser to send money to fund the medical post. The book's gushing and mawkish style is very much of the era; their wounded Belgian patients, for example, are invariably referred to as "dear little soldiers". Yet between the lines the reader gets a glimpse of the daily horror facing both these extraordinary young women. Here, Elsie has to deal with a soldier who has had half his head blown off by a shell:

> "Suddenly a little soldier came to our open door and told me, with tears in his eyes, that a comrade had been terribly badly injured... I saw at once that the poor brave little soldier was past my aid. I said to his comrades *'Il est mort.'* [He is dead.] They turned to me with an incredible look, as if I had spoken from inexperience, but I have seen so many – the number runs into thousands – that I could make no mistake. Poor comrades! They looked so sad and heartbroken... Here was a laughing, cheerful healthy man, one short quarter of an hour ago, and now still and silent, and past all pain."

It was a miracle Elsie and Mairi managed to survive unscathed for as long as they did. But, after three and a half years, their luck ran out. During the late winter of 1918, a cloud of mustard and arsenic gas was sent over to the Belgian trenches from the German lines, and it enveloped Pervyse. Both women were badly affected, especially Elsie. She was evacuated to England, where she stayed for the last six months of the war. Mairi returned to the post to work alone, but she was gassed again a few weeks before the war ended. Gas rarely killed its victims outright. Instead, those worst affected died a lingering death in the decades after the war, their corrupted lungs fighting a long, losing battle against the corrosive chemicals they had inhaled. Others often suffered its effects for the rest of their lives.

Both women made a determined recovery and survived the war. But, like many wartime romances, Elsie's marriage to the baron did not last. They separated in 1919. When war broke out again in 1939, she joined the Women's Auxiliary Air Force (WAAF), and devoted much of her life to fundraising for the RAF Benevolent Fund. She died in 1974. Mairi Chisholm also joined the WAAF, and later became a pioneer racing driver. Following her injury from gas, she suffered from fragile health for the rest of her life, but this did not stop her from living to the ripe old age of 85.

Nightmare at Belleau Wood

1918

The year before the Americans entered the war, the United States had a small army of barely 100,000 men. US president Woodrow Wilson had mixed feelings about committing his country to the conflict. Many American citizens were European immigrants, who had fled to the New World partly to avoid wars like the one currently tearing their old countries apart. Also, a sizable proportion of America's immigrants were from Germany, further complicating any decision about which side to support.

In January 1917, Germany's military commanders decided to allow their U-boats to sink any ship found in British waters. Inevitably, this led to the loss of American cargo ships and the occasional passenger liner, too. This shifted public opinion in America from wary neutrality to a more anti-German outlook. Wilson guessed the time was right; so in April 1917, the United States finally joined the war on the side of the Allies.

Once the Americans had joined the conflict, they set about preparing to prove themselves on the world stage with all the enthusiasm of the bright, upcoming and immensely prosperous nation they had recently become. By the time the war ended in November 1918, there were four million US citizens in the armed forces, and three and three-quarter million of them had been transported over to Europe. They came packed like sardines, in liners hurriedly transformed into troopships. Here, men slept in steel and wire bunk beds placed four on top of each other. The journey was so bad that many soldiers later remarked the trenches that awaited them were more comfortable.

The Germans knew America joining the Allies would make their own victory far more unlikely. Yet in 1917 the war was going Germany's way. Russia, in the throes of revolution, was desperate to make peace, which would end fighting on the Eastern Front. Germany prepared to turn its full attention to the Western Front, intending to sweep away the exhausted French and British armies with the full force of its previously divided army.

At the beginning of 1918, American troopships with newly trained soldiers began to arrive in France, but there were still only a few thousand American troops in Europe. It took time, after all, to raise and prepare a fighting force almost from scratch, and to transport huge numbers of men across the Atlantic. The German generals knew that to win in the West, they would have to strike hard before the Americans arrived in unstoppable numbers. At the end of March, in a carefully planned attack known as the Ludendorff Offensive, German troops broke through the Allied front lines. Part of their success was due to a new tactic. They made surprise attacks to discover their enemy's weak spots, then broke through in strength when they found them.

Throughout the spring, the German armies made a series of extraordinary advances, causing panic among British and French forces. In April, British commander-in-chief Field Marshal Haig issued the desperate order: "With our backs to the wall, and believing in the justice of our cause, each one of us must fight to the end."

Haig feared the loss of the French and Belgian Channel ports, from which troops and supplies were easily transported from Britain to its army on the Western Front. The threat to the French was even more drastic. By early June, the German army had reached the River Marne and the town of Château-Thierry, barely 70km (40 miles) from Paris. As roads became clogged with French civilians fleeing from the fighting, exhausted and demoralized troops melted away, unable to find the will to fight the tidal wave of German troops that welled up before them.

In these desperate circumstances, the British and French generals turned to the American Expeditionary Force (AEF), the first wave of American troops to arrive in Europe, to save the situation. The AEF was under the command of General John J. Pershing. He was well aware that his British and French allies had all but lost the will to wage the war. So the burden of winning was now mainly on the shoulders of his fresh and enthusiastic troops. Yet, so far, Pershing had found commanding his army in Europe to be an unexpectedly frustrating experience. Rather than welcoming the Americans as equal partners, the British and French generals had persistently talked down to Pershing and his staff. They assumed the Americans were naïve and inexperienced – which of course they were. In particular, the Europeans believed that American soldiers would not really have the courage and motivation to fight. One of Pershing's staff remembers the American commander-in-chief banging his fists on the table in a rage and shouting, "I am certainly going to jump down the throat of the next person who asks me 'Will the Americans really fight?' "

The fault for this lack of understanding and trust between the three sides did not entirely lie with the Europeans. Throughout the war, British and French generals had fought together as allies. The Americans, on President Wilson's insistence, did not wish to be considered allies, preferring the term "co-belligerents". They intended to fight alongside the French and British, but not with them. But this situation changed for the better during the Ludendorff Offensive. Drastic, combined action was called for. For the duration of the crisis, all the Allied forces were placed under the control of the veteran French commander, Marshal Ferdinand Foch.

It was in May 1918 that American soldiers first engaged the German army in heavy fighting, at the small village of Cantigny, near the River Somme. Over a third of the American forces there were killed or injured in three days of intense combat – more than enough to prove they were capable of fighting with as much determination as anyone.

At the end of May, Pershing was asked to send soldiers to plug a weak spot in the Allied lines at the town of Château-Thierry. As the German army approached, French troops had fled along with a desperate stream of terrified civilians, clogging the roads away from the town. The nearest American soldiers, the 2nd and 3rd Divisions, were 160 km (100 miles) away. The Americans had to make an exhausting overnight journey, and were expected to begin fighting as soon as they got there. As they approached their destination, the roads became thicker with fleeing French troops and civilians. "You're too late," they kept shouting at the Americans, which can hardly have helped to boost their confidence.

When they arrived in the almost deserted town on June 1, the Americans found a small number of African troops defending it – left behind by their French colonial masters to fight and die in a seemingly impossible situation. Now, they were joined by 17,000 American troops, from both the army and the marines. When the Germans arrived, the battle for the town was intense, but the Americans held on. Fighting turned instead to the nearby town of Lucy-le-Bocage, close to Belleau Wood – a dense, almost impenetrable area of forest and rock around a mile long, and half a mile deep. Belleau Wood had no particular value in itself, but German troops had set up defensive positions there over June 2 and 3. It was proving to be a particularly effective base from which to harass the Americans, so army commanders decided that the Germans had to be driven out – especially as machine gun fire from positions cleverly hidden in the thick undergrowth was causing high casualties.

It had already been a hard battle for the Americans. The whole time they had been in Château-Thierry it had not stopped raining. Artillery fire had fallen on them constantly, and German planes frequently swooped down from the sky to strafe them. It was difficult to shake off the feeling that they were facing a foe far superior in strength and experience.

In many ways, the German troops were much better. They had the most vital advantage any soldier can have – experience. But the Americans were out to prove themselves. They were fresh, well-armed and determined to win. When a French senior officer suggested to Colonel Wendell C. Neville, commander of the 5th Marines, that his men should withdraw, Neville spat: "Retreat? Hell, we just got here."

His marines had had a particularly difficult journey to the Château-Thierry battlefront and, for many of them, it would be their first time in combat. They had been dropped at Meaux station, 30km (20 miles) from the fighting, and had then had to march for two hours uphill. All around them, French artillery batteries fired a continuous barrage over to the German lines, and the ground shook constantly. Neville's men were exhausted, drenched from the rain, and had not been able to wash or shave for days.

Eventually, they arrived at a rendezvous point and were transferred to trucks which carried them towards Château-Thierry. Once there, they were sent to the nearby town of Lucy-le-Bocage, right next to Belleau Wood. Above the woods they spotted German observation balloons (which they nicknamed "sausages" because of their elongated shape). This was not good news. Certain they had been spotted, they awaited their enemy's attentions.

One marine private, William Francis, noted his thoughts about the place in his diary: "The Germans are shelling us pretty hard and the town is practically destroyed...A building on our right is burning, and as the flames light up the ground around us I can see dead marines lying in the narrow road..." Then his

battalion was ordered into Belleau Wood itself:
"At three o' clock [a.m.] we started again for
the front trenches. We must reach the front
lines before daylight. The woods we are
going through is [sic] very dense, it seems
impossible to make our way through, the
limbs of the trees are hitting us in the face
and the men are cursing like the devil...After
a miserable night of hiking we reached the
front-line trenches... The Germans are
shelling us very hard; a shell hit close by
caving in our dug-out. A friend by the name
of Burke was just killed, a piece of shrapnel
taking his head off."

The trenches his fellow soldiers found themselves
in were barely waist-high. After their exhausting day,
men had to try to sleep while crouching ankle-deep
in water.

Over the next couple of days, the Germans
launched night attacks on the newly arrived
Americans. Francis recorded that they were attacked
throughout the hours of darkness. On one occasion,
a soldier threw a grenade at the approaching
Germans, only to have it bounce off a tree and land
back in his trench: "... we saw it just in time to hit the
bottom of our trench and keep from getting killed. I
could hardly keep from laughing for the boy on the
other side of me started cursing because he came
near to getting killed by one of our own men."

On June 6, marines were involved in a particularly costly assault on the woods, when they were ordered to charge against well-defended German positions over an open field. Pinned down by heavy fire during this attack, marine veteran Sergeant Dan Daly had inspired his men with the winning phrase: "Come on ya sons of ****, ya wanna live for ever?" A journalist had been on hand to capture the moment. Daly's immortality in Marine Corps folk law was assured. Such gung-ho bravery in the face of daunting odds was exactly what the marines were supposed to be all about. Daly survived the attack, and the war, although he was wounded in the fighting at Belleau Wood.

What followed was the worst single day's fighting in Marine Corps history, with 1,087 men killed or wounded. But the marines gained a foothold in the woods, and captured the small town of Bouresches on its edge.

Fighting for possession of Belleau Wood took on a grisly, claustrophobic quality. Inside this confined battleground, trees were close together and it was constantly dark. Thick underbrush often covered the ground left between the trees, and there were huge boulders there too, complete with their own little nooks and crannies.

The entire battle was fought in an atmosphere of great confusion. So dense were the woods, it was possible for enemies to pass within a few feet of each other and not see their opponents. In such a place, edgy soldiers had to exercise great care not to shoot their own comrades. As both German and American troops poured into this enclosed place, the ground between the trees became thick with fallen bodies. The personal debris of these dead soldiers – their knapsacks, letters from home and tattered uniforms – all blew around in the wind, pathetic remnants of their young lives, and dark omens for those who were still alive. Hand grenades, machine guns, gas and explosive shells all stripped the leaves from the trees.

When enemies met, it was often in that most dreaded form of fighting, hand–to–hand combat. Men fought with knuckle–dusters, bayonets and a hideous device the marines called a "toad-sticker" – a long, triangular blade attached to a knuckle handle. One marine private, who had been in the thick of hand–to–hand fighting for a terrifying 15 minutes before their surviving German opponents fled, wrote of the awful psychological strain such combat caused. After the fighting, he noted in a letter home, "most of us just sat down and cried."

Having to hold onto such a tightly confined space was an unnerving experience. Shells fell constantly on the American positions, and machine–gun and rifle fire continually sprayed through the trees, raining down chunks of rock, earth and splintered wood on the soldiers. The Germans also fired trench mortars at them – tube–like projectiles 1.3m (4ft) long, packed with high explosives, that the Americans called "aerial torpedoes". They would sail up in the air, stop leisurely at the apex of their short, high arc, and then come crashing down with an explosion that shook all the ground around.

Gas shells also landed in the woods, leaving pockets of highly noxious fumes lurking low on the ground. Usually, the gas dispersed enough to be harmless, but it could catch sleeping or resting marines lying in shallow fox-holes, and leave them choking and retching. On one occasion, in the middle of a gas attack, Gunnery Sergeant Frederick Stockham gave his gas mask to a wounded marine. Stockham died a wretched death a few days later, his lungs destroyed by the gas, but he was posthumously awarded a Medal of Honor in 1939.

When the woods were shelled at night, violent flashes of blue flame would silhouette the splintered tree trunks and branches. Sometimes, said one marine officer, the flashes would come so fast, "it looked as if a great ragged searchlight was playing up and down in the dark." The shell blasts would hammer on the eardrums of the soldiers in the woods, until their ears sang in a constant, disorienting hum. But, more often than not, the shell fire proved ineffective. The blast of the shells was muffled by the density of the trees and vegetation.

With visibility so poor, soldiers on the edge of the woods followed the course of the battles within by listening to a ghastly procession of noises. From time to time, there would be a rapid ripple of machine-gun fire. This could only mean marines were attacking a machine-gun nest, and men were surely dying as they rushed at it. Then there would be an ominous pause, as the machine gunners were killed by bayonets and trench knives – the silent weapons of hand-to-hand fighting.

By June 11, two-thirds of the woods had been captured by the Americans, who were now close to physical exhaustion. But the Germans counter-attacked in force, and intense fighting continued. As corpses piled up inside the woods, marines picked their way past the bodies of their enemy. Sometimes among the dead would be a living soldier, who would rise up behind them to shoot them in the back. The woods were full of snipers, both high in the trees and hidden in the undergrowth. These courageous men, hand-picked for a job that promised almost certain death, were an ever-present hazard when the machine-gunning and shelling died down, and the woods took on a sinister silence.

As if this were not enough, it was easy to get lost in such thick woods. There were few landmarks, and a man could lose all sense of direction. Soldiers had to carry compasses to make sure they returned to their own lines, rather than the enemy's.

On June 23, the Americans withdrew their troops and bombarded the forest for a full 14 hours. Then the soldiers entered again in force, and fought for another two days to try to rid Belleau Wood of

German troops. Fighting was so heavy that 200 ambulances were needed to ferry away the wounded. Eventually, on June 26, Belleau Wood finally fell into American hands. It had taken an agonizing 26 days.

Belleau Wood was one of the most significant battles of the war. If the Americans had not halted the German advance, the Germans could have carried on to Paris. US army general Robert L. Bullard was in no doubt as to the value of these men's achievement: "Had [the marines] arrived a few hours later I think that would have been the beginning of the end – France could not have stood the loss of Paris." The fighting at Belleau Wood was so intense, it also put an end to the speculation about whether American soldiers would really have the heart to fight.

But, for this victory, the marines paid a terrible price. On average, one in three men who took part in the battle was killed or wounded. One company lost 230 of its 250 men.

When the fighting ended, Marine Colonel Frederick May Wise, commander of the second battalion of the 5th Marines, reviewed his men: "At the battle's end... I lined the men up and looked over them. It was enough to break your heart. I had left Courcelles [their previous French position] on May 31 with 965 men and 26 officers – the best battalion I ever saw anywhere. I had taken them, raw recruits for the most. Ten months I had trained them. I had seen them grow into marines. Now before me stood

350 men and six officers; 615 men and 19 officers were gone."

Belleau Wood showed that the American military meant serious business. The Americans would fight a hard war, and casualties would be high, despite the short time they were engaged on the Western Front. By the time the war ended, over 126,000 American troops had lost their lives and 250,000 were wounded.

The American marines were immensely proud of their victory at Belleau Wood. The name is now given to a marine aircraft and troop carrier currently in service in the United States Navy. But, nearly 90 years later, the battle is still a source of controversy and resentment. Some American military historians feel marines should never have been sent into the woods. After all, similar fighting, especially between British and German troops in heavily wooded areas around the Somme and Ypres, had resulted in similarly high casualties. Perhaps American commanders should not have agreed to requests from their French counterparts to clear and hold this dreadful battleground.

Today, Belleau Wood looks as beautiful as any deep forest, and is a popular spot for family picnics. When the sun shines, dappled light plays through the branches, giving a luminous glow to the green moss growing up the trees and a fleeting warmth to the dank, brown carpet of leaves covering the ground.

But, for decades after the fighting there, bodies and unexploded shells continued to be discovered in the forest, and only in their nightmares would visitors venture into the darker depths of Belleau Wood.

From Great War to First World War

1918

Barely a year after the conflict ended, journalist Charles A'Court Repington of the London *Times*, coined the term "The *First* World War". Like many others, he had realized that "the war that will end war" would actually become the major cause of another world war in the future. Even when the warring nations were conducting peace negotiations in Paris in 1919, their leaders knew the peace they were making was not going to last. The French supreme commander, Marshal Ferdinand Foch, dismissed the proceedings as a 20-year cease-fire. British Prime Minister Lloyd George privately remarked: "We shall have to do the whole thing again in 25 years at three times the cost." He was nearly right – the Second World War broke out 20 years later and claimed four times as many lives, rather than three. So the most terrible war in human history had a fitting conclusion – it bred another that would be even worse.

The decision reached in Paris to "make Germany pay" was especially shortsighted. Germany was forced to make payments of billions of dollars, known as "reparations", to the victorious nations. The American delegates, wisely, never agreed to this idea. But France, in particular, insisted on prompt payment.

As the war ended, Germany was hovering on the brink of a communist revolution. Then it suffered the shame of defeat, lost territory and an economy ruined by war and reparations. The German population was outraged. They had won the war in the east, and the war in the west had ended before Allied soldiers invaded Germany. How could it possibly be claimed that they had lost the war? Their bewilderment was especially intense because German newspapers had not reported the full extent of the German army collapse. In the 1930s, a former front-line soldier by the name of Adolf Hitler capitalized on this source of resentment. His Nazi party came to power in 1933 and set in train the events that caused the Second World War.

Men had fought in the war for many reasons. For some, it was duty, patriotism or the belief that they were fighting for a better world. For others, it was the simple fact that they would be imprisoned or shot, and a disgrace to their families, if they didn't. Men who survived the war expected some reward for their efforts. Most were disappointed.

The war left Russia with a Bolshevik government which inflicted famine, murderous purges and severe repression on its population for the next 70 years.

France had won, but it was hardly worth the price. It never recovered its position in the world as a great power. The war left Britain and the British empire with over 942,000 dead and an economy close to breakdown. Only America had done well, emerging as the world's strongest and richest nation.

In another twist of fate, just as the conflict ended, a colossal influenza epidemic swept through the world. Weakened by the stress and deprivation of four years of war, 10 million people died. Among them were William Leefe Robinson, who had shot down the first zeppelin over London, and the now world-famous Austrian painters, Gustav Klimt and Egon Schiele.

Those who survived the war would suffer its consequences for the rest of their lives. Soldiers with lungs ruined by gas, or missing three or even four limbs, slowly faded away in nursing homes. Throughout Europe, asylums were full of men suffering from "shell-shock". Today, this is a psychological condition known and recognized in combat soldiers as post-traumatic stress disorder. But, in 1918, military tradition and society as a whole were only a couple of years on from believing that such men should be shot for cowardice. There are still men and women alive today whose fathers were shot during the war because they suffered mental breakdown brought on by the strain of fighting in the trenches.

Even those who survived with no obvious physical or psychological damage were tormented by what they had seen and done. One in eight men who fought in the war were killed. Most were under 30, and many still in their teens. Hundreds of thousands of women around the same age were unable to marry, because there simply weren't enough men to go around. "When I think I could have been a happy grandmother today if it hadn't been for that terrible war," said one elderly single woman near the end of her life, reflecting a view that must have been held by thousands of others.

The war is now part of our history, and it is still, just about, part of living memory. In 1998, at the 80th anniversary of the armistice, there were 160 men still alive in Britain who had fought in the Great War. Perhaps similar numbers existed in Germany, France, Russia and America. By the time this book is published, almost all of them will have died. The war is still a frequent topic of novels, films and television documentaries. It is difficult to find anything positive to say about it. But perhaps those of that luckless generation born at the end of the 19th century, would take comfort from the fact that the slaughter they endured still haunts us today as a stark reminder of the horror of war.

Sources and further reading

The information in this book came from hundreds of different sources; books, websites, newspaper articles, radio and television documentaries. The author would especially like to acknowledge and recommend the following sources:

General information

The First World War: An Illustrated History by A.J.P. Taylor (Penguin, 1970) is a highly readable account of the conflict by a world famous historian.

The Great War by Correlli Barnett (Penguin, 2000) is another accessible introduction.

The following three books are all haunting first-hand accounts of individuals who fought or lived through the war:

Death's Men – Soldiers of the Great War by Dennis Winter (Penguin, 1978)

1914-1918: Voices and Images of the Great War by Lyn Macdonald (Penguin, 1991)

Voices from the Great War by Peter Vansittart (Pimlico, 1998)

Older readers might like to dip into Paul Fussell's deeply moving *The Great War and Modern Memory* (Oxford University Press, 2000).

The following books were also specifically useful for these chapters:

Chapter 2 – The Angels of Mons

The First Casualty by Phillip Knightley (Prion Books, 2001)

Myths & Legends of the First World War by James Hayward (Sutton Publishing, 2002)

1914: The Days of Hope by Lyn Macdonald (Penguin, 1989)

Chapter 3 – Strange meetings

Silent Night: The Remarkable 1914 Christmas Truce by Stanley Weintraub (Simon and Schuster, 2001)

Chapter 4 – The great zeppelin campaign

Zeppelins of World War One by Wilbur Cross (Paragon House, 1991)

The Zeppelin in Combat by Douglas H. Robinson (Schiffer Publishing Ltd, 1994)

Chapter 5 – The Battle of Jutland

Jutland: The German Perspective by V.E. Tarrant (Cassells and Co., 1995)

The Battleships by Ian Johnston and Rob McAuley (Channel 4 Books, 2000)

Chapter 6 – The first day of the Somme

Somme by Lyn Macdonald (Macmillan, 1983)

1914-1918: Voices and Images of the Great War by Lyn Macdonald (Penguin, 1991), especially for the quote on page 85.

Accrington Pals by William Turner (Wharncliffe Publishing, 1987)

Chapter 8 – The cellar house of Pervyse

The Cellar House of Pervyse: A Tale of Uncommon Things from the Journals and Letters of the Baroness T'Serclaes and Mairi Chisholm (A&C Black, 1917)

The Virago Book of Women and the Great War edited by Joyce Marlow (Virago, 1998)

Chapter 9 – Nightmare at Belleau Wood

The Doughboys – America and the First World War by Gary Mead (Penguin, 2000)

Films

There have been many television documentaries made about the First World War, which make great use of newsreel film shot at the time and of reminiscences of surviving soldiers. There have also been some notable films about the war, although not nearly as many as those made about the Second World War. Here is a small selection of films for you to look out for:

A Month in the Country
Directed by Kenneth Trodd
1987

Based on J.L. Carr's haunting novel, it depicts two English soldiers (played by Colin Firth and Kenneth Branagh) recovering in the country after their time in the trenches.

All Quiet on the Western Front
Directed by Lewis Milestone
1930

This movie version of Erich Maria Remarque's famous novel was made only a couple of years after the advent of talking pictures. It is considered to be one of the most powerful anti-war films ever made.

Gallipoli
Directed by Peter Weir
1981

Mel Gibson and Mark Lee star as two Australian soldiers caught up in the carnage of the Gallipoli landings in 1915.

Lawrence of Arabia
Directed by David Lean
1962

Starring Peter O'Toole as Lawrence of Arabia, this stunning epic depicts one of the lesser known battlegrounds of the First world War – the Middle East.

Oh What a Lovely War
Directed by Richard Attenborough
1969
Laurence Olivier, Maggie Smith, John Gielgud and Ian Holm feature in this musical, which parodies the horrors of the war by making use of the popular songs of the day.

Paths of Glory
Directed by Stanley Kubrick
1957
Kirk Douglas stars as a French officer in this gripping tale of three French soldiers court-martialed for cowardice. The film so offended the French government in its depiction of the incompetence of their most senior officers, that the film was banned in that country for decades.

Regeneration
Directed by Gilles Mackinnon
1997
Based on Pat Barker's famous novel of the same name, this handsome movie features James Wilby and Stuart Bunce as war poets Siegfried Sassoon and Wilfred Owen, recovering from their time in the trenches at Craiglockheart Psychiatric Hospital, Edinburgh.

Poetry of the First World War

The war produced some extraordinary and moving poetry, which can be found in such books as:

Up the Line to Death by Brian Gardner (ed) (Methuen, 1964)

Some Corner of a Foreign Field by James Bentley (ed) (Little, Brown and Co., 1992)

History through Poetry - World War One by Paul Dowswell (Hodder Wayland, 2001)

The Poems of Wilfrid Owen Wordsworth Editions Ltd., 1994

The War Poems of Siegfried Sassoon (Faber & Faber, 1999)

For links to websites, where you can read poems from the First World War online, go to the Usborne Quicklinks Website at www.usborne-quicklinks.com and type in the keywords "first world war". For safe Web surfing, please follow the safety guidelines given on the Usborne Quicklinks Website.

Also from Usborne True Stories

TRUE STORIES OF THE SECOND WORLD WAR

Paul Dowswell

This time two torpedoes hit home. One caused only minor damage. The other went off underneath the stern, with a huge watery explosion that shot like a whiplash through the length of the ship. It buckled deck plates and bulkheads, and threw men to the floor or against metal partitions and instruments, with breathtaking violence. Above the site of the explosion, water surged into the ship with a vengeance, flooding the entire steering compartment.

Epic encounters between titanic warships, battles involving thousands of men, and duels between lone snipers facing almost certain death are just some of the dramatic tales in this gripping collection of stories from the Second World War.

TRUE
ESCAPE
STORIES
Paul Dowswell

Finally, the night had come to take a trip to the roof. Morris spent the day beforehand trying to curb his restlessness. What if the way up to the roof was blocked? What if the ventilator motor had been replaced after all? All their painstaking work would be wasted. The 12-year sentence stretched out before him. Then another awful thought occurred. The holes in the wall would be discovered eventually, and that would mean even more years added on to his sentence.

As well as locked doors, high walls and barbed wire, many escaping prisoners also face savage dogs and armed guards who shoot to kill. From Alcatraz to Devil's Island, read the extraordinary tales of people who risked their lives for their freedom.

TRUE
SURVIVAL
STORIES
Paul Dowswell

As he fell through the floor Griffiths instinctively grabbed at the bombsight with both hands, but an immense gust of freezing air sucked the rest of his body out of the aircraft. With the wind and the throb of the Boston's two engines roaring in his ears, he found himself halfway out of the plane, legs and lower body pressed hard against the fuselage. He yelled at the top of his voice: "Geeeerrrooooowwwww!!!!", but knew immediately that there was almost no chance his crewmate could hear him.

From shark attacks and blazing airships to exploding spacecraft and sinking submarines, these are real stories of people who have stared death in the face and lived to tell the tale. Find out what separates the living from the dead when catastrophe strikes.

Also from Usborne True Stories

TRUE STORIES
OF
HEROES

Paul Dowswell

His blood ran cold and Perevozchenko was seized by panic. He knew that his body was absorbing lethal doses of radiation, but instead of fleeing he stayed to search for his colleague. Peering into the dark through a broken window, he could see only a mass of tangled wreckage. By now he had absorbed so much radiation he felt his whole body was on fire. But then he remembered that there were several other men near to the explosion who might be trapped...

From firefighters battling with a blazing nuclear reactor to a helicopter rescue team on board a fast-sinking ship, this is an amazingly vivid collection of stories about men and women whose extraordinary courage has captured the imagination of millions.

Shortlisted for the Blue Peter Book Awards 2002

TRUE
SPY
STORIES

Paul Dowswell & Fergus Fleming

"In all your years of fame," Kramer explained delicately, "you have known some of the most powerful men in Europe. Would you consider returning to Paris now to mingle again with these influential gentlemen? And, while you're doing this, might you be able to keep me informed of anything interesting they might say?"

Margaretha looked curious but non-committal.

Kramer went on, "We could pay you well for this information − say 24,000 francs."

What are real spies like? Some, like beautiful Mata Hari, are every bit as glamorous as famous fictional agents such as James Bond. But spies usually live shadowy double lives, risking prison, torture and execution for a chance to change history.

Also from Usborne True Stories

TRUE EVEREST ADVENTURES

Paul Dowswell

Tejbir collapsed soon afterwards, telling Finch and Bruce he had no strength to go on. Defeated, he returned to the tent. Then as Finch and Bruce climbed higher, a terrible wind blew up, making progress extremely slow. At 8,320m (27,300ft) disaster struck. Finch, who was leading the climb, suddenly heard Bruce call out in alarm: "I'm getting no oxygen!" Finch turned to see his companion wavering and about to topple off the mountain.

Everest has fascinated climbers ever since it was first discovered 150 years ago. Since then, over a thousand of them have stood triumphant on its summit. But the frozen bodies that litter its slopes tell another tale of tragedy, misfortune and reckless ambition.

Also from Usborne True Stories

TRUE
POLAR
ADVENTURES

Paul Dowswell

By day, they pushed on through towering seas, while men not rowing bailed furiously to keep their open boats afloat. By night, they clambered aboard passing ice floes, to shiver in their tents. But one night there was a loud crack, and the ice split through the middle of a tent. Ernest Holness, one of the *Endurance's* stokers, fell through. He floundered in the freezing sea, trapped in his soaking sleeping bag, stunned almost to paralysis by the shock of the icy water.

Guarded by frozen seas and vast fields of snow, the North and South poles are among the world's most mysterious places. But these bleak environments are no place for humans, as the explorers who set out to unearth their secrets have found to their cost.

Shortlisted for the Blue Peter Book Awards 2003